AMERICAN ART: ITS AWFUL ALTITUDE

A SATIRE

American Artists, ah!
American Patrons, PSHAW!!
American Critics, BAH!!!

by

JOHN FRANKENSTEIN

edited by

WILLIAM COYLE
FLORIDA ATLANTIC UNIVERSITY

Bowling Green University Popular Press
Bowling Green, Ohio 43403

The Bowling Green University Popular Press is the publishing division of the Center for the Study of Popular Culture, Ray B. Browne, Director.

ISBN: 0-87972-037-9

Printed in the United States of America.

American Art:

ITS AWFUL ALTITUDE.

A SATIRE.

American Artists, *ah!*
American Patrons, PSHAW!!
American Critics, BAH!!!.

By JOHN FRANKENSTEIN.

CINCINNATI:
1864.

AMERICAN ART:

ITS AWFUL ALTITUDE.

A SATIRE.

American Artists, *ah!*
American Patrons, PSHAW!!
American Critics, BAH!!!

Old scores to settle,
And sores to heal,
I 'll show my mettle,
And use my heel,
Rough-shod,
By G—d!
To friends departed,
The noble-hearted,
Alive or dead,
Who 've cheered me often,
My words will soften
To love instead.

Written during the Third Year of the Great Rebellion, 1863–4,

By JOHN FRANKENSTEIN.

CINCINNATI, OHIO
1864.

088257

CONTENTS

INTRODUCTION

Most American artists had difficulty supporting themselves by their talents in the 19th century, and the Civil War years were especially lean ones. In 1864, after thirty years of struggling for recognition, John Frankenstein, a painter-sculptor of Cincinnati, published at his own expense *American Art: Its Awful Altitude*, a lengthy Dunciad in which he struck out at persons and institutions that he felt had hampered or undervalued his work. After issuing his blast at the art world of the Queen City, he left for New York and never returned. Violent and sensational though it was, the book did not create the uproar its author apparently expected. The Cincinnati *Gazette* on August 16, 1864, noted briefly that it was a "queer volume" and that "the poetry is like his pictures containing about a tithe of the merit their author supposes them to possess." There is a legend that prominent Cincinnati citizens bought up copies and destroyed them, but it seems more likely that most people simply ignored the book so that Frankenstein was left in the ironical situation of a child who has a tantrum while no one is watching.

From a literary point of view, the poem has little value except to demonstrate that for the creation of effective satire rage is not enough. Psychologically it holds some interest as an outpouring of paranoia. But the doggerel of one century can become social history for the next, and as a historical document the poem has considerable significance. As he slashed out ineptly at real and fancied adversaries, Frankenstein commented on many fellow-artists, suggested something of the active cultural life of Cincinnati in the pre-Civil War years when residents liked to refer to the city as the Athens of the West, and touched on several aspects of the American artist's condition: the public's admiration for grandiose effects in paintings of nature like those of Cole and Church and its lack of enthusiasm for Biblical and mythological subjects treated in the grand style, the uncertain patronage of the wealthy, the greater uncertainty of governmental patronage, disputes over the decoration of the U. S. Capitol, the controversy over nudity in art, the American Art Union and other attempts to interest the public in painting and sculpture, the preference for European artists and for Americans trained in Europe, the effect of photography on portrait painting—the bread and butter of many artists, the dominance of the National Academy of Design, and the superficiality of most journalistic criticism of the arts.

Frankenstein's abusive survey of American art is not all-inclusive, and in fact from the perspective of 1972 some of his omissions are rather surprising. He inveighs against the American Art Union but does not mention two of its most popular artists, Thomas Cole and George Caleb Bingham. He also ridicules the National Academy of Design but does not refer to its president from 1845 to 1861, the landscape painter Asher B. Durand. Except for a reference to Lilly Martin Spencer, he does not discuss domestic genre scenes, the subject matter most popular with the general public during the years when he was struggling to succeed with portraits and "Christ pictures." He criticises the decoration of the U. S. Capitol, which was a source of much public controversy, but does not mention the uproar in the 1840s over Horatio Greenough's colossal statue of George Washington in the costume and general posture of Phidias' "Zeus." Thomas Crawford's statue "Armed Victory" was hoisted atop the Capitol dome on December 2, 1863, while Frankenstein was composing his satire; if he had known that Jefferson Davis, while Secretary of War, had caused a feathered headdress to be substituted for the liberty cap worn by freed Roman slaves, his antipathy toward the Confederacy would certainly have induced him to include this incident. Although he was active in Philadelphia art circles in the early 1840s, he does not refer to Thomas Sully, John Sartain, John Neagle, or any of the numerous descendants of Charles Willson Peale. So many artists worked in Cincinnati during the 1840s and 1850s that Frankenstein could scarcely have mentioned them all. Among his more surprising omissions are the sculptor Henry Kirke Brown, who intended to become a painter until Nicholas Longworth's advice prompted his "dropping the brush and wielding the chisel"; Miner K. Kellogg, the painter who served as Hiram Powers' agent and defender during the highly profitable exhibition tour of "The Greek Slave"; William L. Sonntag, a pupil of his brother Godfrey; and three distinguished painters, all of whom he must have known: T. Worthington Whittredge, Joseph Oriel Eaton, and Eastman Johnson. Selective though Frankenstein's satire is, it sheds some garish and erratic light on the world of American art in the middle third of the 19th century.

****

John Frankenstein was the eldest of a family of six children, all of whom became artists. Precise information concerning them is scarce because they are in a kind of limbo between oblivion and obscurity. They are treated only in the most inclusive biographical encyclopedias of artists, and occasional newspaper references, even their obituaries, are filled with contradictions and inaccuracies. Some fresh minutia have come to light in manuscript diaries kept by Dr. James Lakey between 1848 and 1854. These diaries, recently acquired by the Cincinnati Historical Society, contain numerous references to the Frankensteins. Dr. Lakey knew the entire family for more than twenty years and often recorded that one of the sisters had called to read aloud to him or to ask his advice on medical and family problems. John frequently quarreled with other members of the family and turned up at Dr. Lakey's office to spend the night. Both the physician and the artist apparently led somewhat Bohemian lives. On December 30, 1848, Dr. Lakey noted in his diary that John's "health suffers from intemperance and debauchery." On June 14, 1849, along with four other Cincinnati citizens, Frankenstein signed a statement "exonerating" Dr. Lakey from related charges of seduction and abortion.

Another difficulty in studying the Frankensteins results from the fact that they were volatile eccentrics, individualistic and often stubbornly perverse—the kind of persons whose behavior encourages legends so that it often is difficult to separate the actual from the apocryphal.

The father, John A. Frankenstein (Nov. 13, 1789-May 29, 1842), seems to have set the pattern of arrogance and vanity later followed by his children. Born in Raidelbach, Germany, he was well educated for a man of his day.

He became schoolmaster, choir leader, and church organist in a nearby parish, probably Worfelden. There he married the charming and talented daughter of a moderately wealthy man, Anna Katherine Volhart (Nov. 9, 1791-Jan. 26, 1871), and there his six children were born. Losing his position in 1831 apparently motivated his emigration to America. One story is that he was discharged because the conservative pastor disapproved of his correspondence with August Follen, a political radical living in Switzerland. A more prosaic legend is that one of his duties was to post the hymns at the front of the church and when he persisted in overruling the pastor's selections and substituting hymns of his own choice, he was relieved of his duties. John Frankenstein's family name was actually Tracht. One legend concerning his change of name is that after coming to America he was dismayed to hear Americans pronounce it as though it were *Dreck* (filth), but it seems unlikely that this happened very often in Cincinnati, where there were many German residents. A more tenable explanation is that before leaving Germany he won a prize for an oil painting of the ruins of Frankenstein Castle. His pride in this painting led him to assume the name Frankenstein, which his family used thereafter.

The arrival of the Frankensteins in the New World was a dramatic one. Approximately 150 members of the Tracht family sailed from Bremen on July 14, 1831, aboard the British ship *Dove*, bound for Baltimore. On September 16 a storm drove the ship from its course, and it struck a sandbar off the coast of Virginia. The Tracht men forced the crew to remain aboard and operate the pumps, and when the storm cleared the passengers were removed to shore. September 17, the day of their rescue, was afterward observed by members of the Tracht family as a day of thanksgiving. The various family groups dispersed into Pennsylvania and Ohio. John Frankenstein apparently took his wife and six children directly to Cincinnati, where one of his sisters had settled the year before. Because he was unwilling or unable to learn English, he could not resume his teaching career. Working as an apprentice under John Geyer, he learned cabinetmaking and supported his family by working at this trade until his death in 1842. All six of his children were artistically gifted. In 1849 the family moved to Springfield, Ohio; in 1893 the surviving sisters and one brother returned to Cincinnati.

Godfrey Nicholas (Sept. 8, 1820-Feb. 24, 1873) began painting signs in Cincinnati at an early age. Apparently the "good son" of the family, he was the chief support of his mother and sisters. He painted a great many landscapes, portraits, and family groups. In 1847 he made his first excursion to the White Mountains and he returned to the region on several later occasions, sometimes with one of his sisters; his last visit was in 1871. His paintings of the scenery around Crawford Notch led residents to name a rugged rock formation Frankenstein Cliff, and when a railway bridge was later constructed it was called Frankenstein Trestle. In 1867 he made his only trip to Europe and painted a number of mountain scenes in the Swiss Alps. From 1840 until his death, however, his favorite subject was Niagara Falls (see Plate I). An article entitled "Niagara" by A. H. Guernsey in *Harper's* for August, 1853, reproduced seventeen of his "studies" of the Falls and praised his work but did not identify him. Besides a hundred or more separate paintings, he created for public exhibition a panorama on a strip of canvas one thousand feet long and nine feet high. As this huge canvas unrolled from one spindle to another, he would read a lecture about the scenes that appeared. The panorama was first shown in New York City in mid-July, 1853, and was afterward exhibited in cities throughout the United States.

George Leo (June 26, 1825-Sept. 15, 1911) worked on several newspapers in the Midwest and in 1875 moved to New York, where he edited *Turf, Field and Farm.* In 1866 he wrote Secretary of State Seward asking him to support his ambitious project of painting famous scenes of the Civil War. Five of his paintings are now displayed at Appomattox Court House National Park. He died in a home for the aged in Poughkeepsie, New York. Gustavus Ludwig (*c.*1829-Dec. 11, 1893) may have been the most eccentric of the Frankensteins. He moved with his sisters to Springfield, and his name appears in the city directories with various designations: artist, teacher, mathematician, and horologist. He lived alone in a small studio and clockmaking shop that he built on the family lot. According to Dr. Isaac Kay of Springfield, whose recollections of the family were published in the local newspaper in 1915, Gustavus quarreled with his sisters and went to the Sandwich Islands, where the natives burned his hut and threatened to kill him. He specialized in floral paintings, but his major interest, which became an obsession, was mathematics. He lectured on the relationships of numbers and in 1875 published a pamphlet, *Magic Reciprocals.* His method was to begin with a magic square or cube and then to devise a visual representation of the numbers by means of a geometrical diagram. The results, he wrote, are "emblematic of the glory of the universe."

Marie Magdalena Catharina (Nov. 20, 1822 -Feb. 28, 1900) is a somewhat mysterious figure. Her marriage to Alfred D. Coombs may have been the reason for the family's removal to Springfield. She sued unsuccessfully for a divorce after a few months of marriage. Although Dr. Lakey testified in her behalf, he found her complaints about her husband tedious and began referring to her in his diary as "the weariful woman." She is listed as an artist in Springfield city directories, and like Godfrey and Elizabeth she taught at the Springfield Female Seminary. Although she gave her age as sixty-five in 1907, Elizabeth (*c.*1828-May 3, 1919) was probably born in 1828, because Dr. Lakey describes her as six years younger than Marie, and he first knew the girls when they were three and nine years old. She is listed as an artist and as a teacher in Springfield directories. She was Godfrey's favorite and accompanied him on many of his sketching excursions. Henry Howe, who toured Ohio in the mid-1880s gathering material for a new edition of his *Historical Collections of Ohio*, describes her coming to the door "with pallet and brush in hand, an earnest, busy little woman . . . . almost too much absorbed in her painting even to talk." She told Howe that her brother Godfrey was not only the best landscape painter in America but "the greatest the world ever knew." On July 15, 1907, she attempted suicide by jumping into the Ohio River in Cincinnati. According to the Cincinnati *Enquirer*, she answered police officers' questions "haughtily." The newspaper headline read DESPAIRED OF SELLING HER PICTURES AND SOUGHT DEATH BY DROWNING TO END HER WOE. One legend is that, angered by the public's indifference, she destroyed her brothers' letters and paintings. She spent her last years in a Methodist home for the aged in Cincinnati.

It would be sentimental futility to describe the Frankensteins as geniuses stifled by a society indifferent to the fine arts, but they were earnest and dedicated artists. The most talented and the most pathetic in his struggle for recognition was the eldest, John Peter (Dec. 19, 1817-April 16, 1881). Gifted musically and artistically, he was playing the piano and drawing pictures when he was seven years old. Soon after the family arrived in Cincinnati, he started working for an engraver. His parents encouraged him to continue in this profession, but he decided to become a portrait painter, and in 1834 at the age of seventeen he rented a studio in Foote's Row (see Plate II), where cubicles were available at low rents. In 1837 he moved to a studio in the Mechanics' Institute. Like many artists of the time, he learned artistic techniques by observing and imitating older artists, but he may have received some instruction and encouragement from Friedrich Eckstein, who taught the young sculptor Hiram Powers. Frankenstein painted portraits of several prominent Kentucky residents between 1836 and 1839. In 1839 he went to Philadelphia, where he became a close friend of Willis Gaylord Clark (Oct. 5, 1808-June 12, 1841), editor of the Philadelphia *Gazette*, who sat for a portrait (see Plate III) and arranged for him to make a portrait bust of William H. Seward, the newly elected Governor of New York.

John Frankenstein lived in Philadelphia from 1839 to 1844. His movements during the next ten years cannot be pinpointed; he spent some time in Canada, in New York, in Washington, and perhaps in Boston and returned intermittently to Cincinnati. On May 19, 1853, he missed an appointment with Dr. Lakey because he had no watch; the doctor commented in his diary "He is 37 years old and poor! Imprudence the cause." The following day Frankenstein told Dr. Lakey that he would like to trade some of his paintings for a piano. On June 30, 1854, the doctor wrote that he had visited John in his fourth floor studio: "He lives on bread and molasses and drinks hydrant water! His expense is 34 cents a week!" In his poem Frankenstein hints that some of his difficulties had resulted from intemperance. On July 30, 1854, William Miller, a Cincinnati artist, wrote to a friend:

> Frankenstein is here again, and a totally changed man of sober habits, and as an artist extremely enthusiastic. His style is coming back to what it was in his best days, and I believe he will yet do something that will make the people open their eyes with more than mere wonder.
>
> (Cincinnati Historical Society)

From 1856 to 1864 he is listed in Cincinnati directories at 14 East Fourth Street. In November, 1864, he arrived in New York City, where he apparently remained for the rest of his life. In 1866 he published two letters signed Frank Ensten in the New York *Post*. The letter of May 5, attacking the exhibition at the National Academy of Design, contained a characteristic gibe:

Oh dear,
How they smear,
Worse each year!

His name has not been discovered again in New York newspapers until April 17, 1881, when they carried long accounts of his death. He had lived for several years as a hermit in a small frame house on Long Island. In late March he sent for a doctor, whom he informed that he was suffering from nervous shock because a plaster model on which he was working had fallen and broken. The doctor called several times thereafter, and on April 16 when no one answered his knock, he sent for the police, who broke down the door and found John Frankenstein dead.

****

The scraps of available biographical information regarding John Frankenstein combine into a series of pathetic contrasts. For example, around 1838, using himself or Godfrey as a model, he painted "The Artist in His Studio" (see Plate IV). The intent young man, sketching at his work table while surrounded by his paintings and works of sculpture, represents his idealized conception of the artist. In grim antithesis, forty-two years later his neighbors described him to reporters as "an old man with long gray curling hair and a ragged gray beard" who never spoke to anyone. When police broke open the door of his house, they entered a dark, squalid room littered with newspapers, books, wood ashes from the stove, and trash. Paintings, sketches, and busts, covered with dust and cobwebs, were stacked everywhere. In one corner were the stereotype plates for *American Art: Its Awful Altitude.* Boards had been laid across the frame of an old couch, and there Frankenstein's body was sprawled. He wore a red flannel shirt, black pants, and rubber shoes. Beside the body was a half-finished plaster bust of Goethe covered with a white cloth.

The Seward papers in University of Rochester Library contain several references to John Frankenstein. In his autobiography William H. Seward describes him as "a young sculptor, erect and fine looking, with dark curly hair." During the winter of 1839 Mrs. Seward often mentioned him in letters to her sister. She wrote that he was "extremely diffident" but was her son's favorite companion; he read Shakespeare to young Fred Seward and romped with him in the snow. In September of 1840 Frankenstein wrote to Seward that he had called at the family home in Auburn and taken away his bust of Mrs. Seward so that he could finish it in Philadelphia. In 1846 when Seward was touring the West and visited Cincinnati, he wrote his wife that he found Frankenstein still working on the bust. On May 25, 1852, Frankenstein sent Seward a coldly formal letter asking that $75 or $100 be sent him immediately. Like most of Frankenstein's relationships with other people, this one seems to have ended in bitterness.

On November 19, 1864, the New York *Times* reported the arrival of "the distinguished Western artist Frankenstein." On December 3 his landscapes were lauded in extravagant terms for their "brilliancy and purity of color and tones, so accurately graduated, in relative proportion to nature, as to produce a wonderful stereoscopic effect." His painting of Niagara Falls "ushers in a new era in the art history of the world . . . is a scientific as well as an artistic success." His bust of the Cincinnati surgeon Reuben D. Mussey (June 23, 1780-June 21, 1866) "proves that in sculpture he is equal to his power in paint." Presumably this was the bust on which Frankenstein was working at the time of his death. His obituary in the New York *Sun* quoted from his letter to William H. Mussey, the doctor's son:

> The model has done its own work of casting by casting itself on the floor. The head is completely severed from the rest, and there is a big split in it besides. It fell forward. Ten seconds later and I would have set a new fashion of hari-kari, for the 298 pounds of solid clay would have fallen on me and crushed me. Say nothing of my misfortune to any one. I'll go immediately and make another model.

****

The footnotes following the text of the poem identify most of Frankenstein's allusions. As the poem amply demonstrates, however, his animosities required very slight provocation; the motivation behind some of his attacks and even the identity of a few of his targets, such as his landlord and the Cincinnati photographer he calls "Baby-booby," remain mysterious. Nevertheless, the intrinsic interest of the poem and its relevance to American art history seem to justify its being made more widely available despite some regrettable lacunae in the annotation.

I first encountered a tattered copy of *American Art: Its Awful Altitude* in the Martha Kinney Cooper Ohioana Library, Columbus; I am grateful to Walter Rumsey Marvin, Director Emeritus, and to Beatrice Williams Foley, the present Director, for the use of the text and for the opportunity to work in that library's unique collection of Ohio-related material. The investigation of a relatively obscure person like John Frankenstein has entailed my addressing requests and queries, many of them seemingly inconsequential, to hundreds of librarians, archivists, museum directors, and scholars. To list everyone whose time and patience I have abused would be impossible, but I wish to express special gratitude to Yeatman Anderson, III, Cincinnati Public Library; Margaret B. Andrews, University of Rochester Library; Dorothy T. Cullen, Filson Club Library, Louisville, Kentucky; Edward H. Dwight, Director, Munson-Williams-Proctor Institute, Utica, New York; Luella Eutsler, Wittenberg University Library; Jeanne Henning, Florida Atlantic University Library; Alice Hook, Cincinnati Art Museum; Lee Majors, Cincinnati Historical Society; Garnett McCoy, Archives of American Art, Washington, D.C.; James G. McCulla, Florida Atlantic University Photo Laboratory; Mary M. Miller, Warder Public Library, Springfield, Ohio; Dean Jack Suberman, College of Humanities, Florida Atlantic University; Carl Vitz, Director Emeritus, Cincinnati Public Library; and Louise Wallman, Pennsylvania Academy of the Fine Arts, Philadelphia. I am, as always, most deeply grateful for the patience and encouragement of my wife, Charlotte Coyle. My research was supported in part by a grant from the Florida Atlantic University Division of Sponsored Research.

William Coyle
Florida Atlantic University

EXPLANATORY.

As I may possibly have readers not acquainted with our town and its history, I would state to them that the erection of the Pioneer Monument, and, of course, the delivery of the speech of Billem Sorry, Esq., are pure fictions. The Pioneer Association accepted a secondhand design offered by Tremendous Dead Bones, Esq., Sculptor; but with this effort their monumental energies expired. Aside, however, from his allusions to this erection, the speech by Billem Sorry, Esq., deals in nothing but facts, except that the ancient maiden of the Ladies' Academy of the Fine Arts is also an invention, and that the hoops of the fat member may appear a year or so before the fashion.

None of the facts and opinions, none of the likes and dislikes it contains, are Billem Sorry's, but my own—all except the sublime self-conceit; that is Billem Sorry's. To exhibit this in its perfection I was obliged to resort to the machinery I have employed.

The other statements in the poem affecting real persons are literally true. Where an individual is speaking in the first person, all the words used, placed within quotation marks, are actual quotations from the mouth of that person.

The names also are all real but those in the list below. I changed these only because such was my whim. In order to be strictly impartial, but chiefly because I want the real names to be known, I give them opposite the nickname in the order they appear.

Nickname.	Real name.
TREMENDOUS DEAD BONES, Esq., Sculptor.	THOS. D. JONES, Esq., Sculptor.
BILLEM SORRY, Esq.,	WM. M. CORRY, Esq., Democratic *copperhead* politician.
NICK LITTLEWORTH,	The late NICHOLAS LONGWORTH, Millionaire of Cincinnati.

BILLY 'DAMS, ... WM. A. ADAMS, (5)

Who lives on the east side of Broadway, below Fourth street, Cincinnati; the same who heads the list of *honorary* members of the New York National Academy of Design.

An urgent—almost importunate—request induces me to leave out of this list a name already written for the printer; the request extended to the text—but that I will not give up. The papers of to-day (March 15) give additional proof of the correctness of one at least of the amiable characteristics imputed to him. (6)

PRETTY POPKINS, ... L. C. HOPKINS, (7)

Dry goods merchant, at the N. E. corner of Fifth and Vine streets, Cincinnati.

MR. PHILIPPS, ... R. C. PHILLIPS, a surveyor. (8)

SCRATCH-CLUB, ... SKETCH-CLUB. (9

Though an actual person, I pass by Baby-booby; let me say, however, emphatically, that I do *not* mean Mr. ——, his partner. (10

My landlord's name I leave out, by particular request.

I could heartily have wished that Wm. Page, E. Leutze, T. Buchanan Read and Geo. L. Brown, with all of whom my personal relations have been pleasant, had not compelled me to write regarding them as I have done. That they are prominently before the public, that they could prove ability did they but choose to exert it, makes the case only the worse and my duty the more imperative.

I have had no grand intention of improving the existing condition of Art. I wrote only because I wanted to write. My brother having disposed of my large picture, Series of Niagara No. 2, by subscription—not with that intention, however—I am enabled to print and publish this on my sole responsibility.

After the publication of this work I shall be prepared to find myself depicted as a monster of crime, folly and vices. Should there be any who would wish to busy themselves in this way, let them use their pleasure.

Those who wish to address me will please direct to Station D, New York City.

CINCINNATI, OHIO, *March* 15, 1864.

DEDICATORY.

CINCINNATI, OHIO, *Oct.* 3, 1863.

MR. WM. H. COMSTOCK, 14 *and* 16 *West Pearl st., Cincinnati, Ohio:*

MINE ANCIENT FRIEND—Please find inclosed the Ten Dollars ($10 00) I borrowed of you some months ago. When I first asked you to lend it to me, I requested the loan for one month; on the day that month expired, you were not in when I came to your store. I went there again the next day, desiring you to extend the time, stating, however, distinctly that I had the money with me (having borrowed it elsewhere) to pay you *then*. You acceded to my second request. Since no specified time was mentioned on the last occasion, and learning that you had a conversation with my brother George on the subject, I deemed it unnecessary to say anything more until I was able and willing to redeem the debt.

When I first borrowed this money of you, a man whom we both have known long had promised, within a very short time, to pay me a part of what he owed me; he is a first-rate fellow, yet he failed to keep his promise; not only that, he has voluntarily promised again since, but I have not, to this moment, received a cent from him. I am satisfied, however, that he can not very well help it.

Perhaps you do not know how much I am constantly disappointed and vexed in my little money-matters. Although I have for a long time in this city, faithfully and diligently labored to do good work in several branches of painting and sculpture; although I have carefully avoided having a family on my hands; although I have reduced my own wants to what is absolutely necessary; never even using whisky or tobacco in any form, the first of which, at least, you enjoy in such abundance: still, I get so little to do, and that little is in most cases so long being paid for, while in other instances it is not paid for at all, that I am never free from petty though vexatious embarrassments.

Something over a year ago, the idea became distinct in my brain that my old boyhood friend, Wm. H. Comstock, had gathered of the goods of this world so as to be wealthy. I thought that he, being probably not aware of the diminutive though dogging difficulties with which I was beset, would, were the case presented to him, order work for two or three hundred dollars; would interest himself to get ten or twelve of his wealthy friends to do likewise; thus obtaining for me, certainly a very moderate sum, yet one sufficient, if invested, to relieve me so that I could continue my work in comparative peace.

I also thought, and think now, when a man has thus diligently labored for many years in a community, that his cotemporaries, particularly his personal acquaintances, whose labor is naturally more productive of money, should, not in the way of charity, but on the broad ground of human, cosmopolitan civilization, sustain an honest perseverance in the Fine Arts, in the same way as other departments of human cultivation are so nobly sustained among us; that work, requiring the qualities of a man of refinement, might be produced at least without the harrowing hell of the doubt of daily supplies of necessaries. Whatever the merit of my work may be, I can claim the honest and persevering endeavor always to do it as well as I could.

It does not pay. I have tried it long, as you know, or ought to know. I am now straining all my faculties to get into another business, wherein I hope to find a decent living.

In writing my autobiography, I shall tell how almost singly your conduct toward me was distinguished; how, in a city where I had passed almost my whole life, and where I was four or five years ago only a whole year and a half without any employment, I found at last a friend who lent me, somewhat grudgingly it must be confessed, the sum of TEN DOLLARS! who, when my brother applied to him for a subscription to my picture, Series of Niagara, No. 2, supposing it to be a dollar, handed a dollar to him; but on being informed that each subscription was ten dollars, indignantly refused to have anything to do with it, telling my brother that I already owed him thirty dollars—three times the real amount, to be sure—yet proving that he loved to enlarge the lousy littlenesses of life, and that he could possibly even be brought eventually to imagine he had given me an order for a picture worth three hundred dollars, and had paid it in advance—it being more easy to change 30 into 300 than 10 into 30; besides, having to his previous wealth, added a fortune made out of the misfortunes of his country, he could now at any rate afford to *talk* more liberally.

Should this additional hallucination—giving me an order for a three hundred dollar picture, with payment in advance—take possession of you, I will with great pleasure mention it in my autobiography; let it be distinctly understood, however, that this is by no means necessary to enable me to speak in such terms of your generosity as its immensity demands.

I have witnesses to prove that I inclosed Ten dollars to your address.

Of late, when we pass in the street, you do not speak, but glare, as if you would make me feel horrible; perhaps this letter will indicate how you succeed in that awful demonstration.

CONTENTS.

PART IV.

PART I.

THE man who lives in earnest is a fool;
Humbugs are wise and use him as a tool;
They, like a fungus, from the Real grow,
Misshape its form and while few care or know,
They get the cash, the finest women, all
That is worth having since old Adam's fall.

'T is well to live, till you can learn to laugh,
Of other worlds this must be the riffraff—
A lesson hard to get, to bear its weight;
Most difficult the choice, to laugh or hate;
But caustic mirthfulness will soon become,
A pleasant friend, an entertaining chum.

I fell in with the Fine Arts when a boy;
Some friendly warnings did not wish me joy;
And paint! long, patient service thou hast met,
By giving me no decent living yet.
All sorts of pictures I have tried to daub,
They sell not, and I seldom get a job.
I also am a man who makes mudpates—
The President of the United States,
Thus designated T. D. BONES, Esquire,
Sculptor, and can authority be higher?

(Tremendous Dead Bones, Esquire, Sculptor, makes
Lines so uncouth that every fiber quakes)
To Father Abraham, whom heaven defend,
Bones sends a note to introduce his friend—
"Bones! Bones! I don't know Bones!" the poor man says—
Oppressed by treason's and corruption's ways—
"Bones! Bones! Oh yes! confound those curst Confeds—
It's—it's—that man out West that makes mud heads!"
That makes mud heads! Bones! grin! nay, be not sore!
From Adam down, what has the Lord done more?

I court the scribbling muse now; worse and worst?
Ah! am I then by all the Fates accurst?
Nay, nay, to my first love I but return,
I wooed her when a child, once more I burn
For her, of all my friends, first, last, and best;
She urges me to work, gives me no rest;
No fear, no faith, her froward mind enchains,
Nor hope of heaven—hell's penalties and pains—
Much less the evil men may here inflict,
Affright her will, that I must truth depict.
Thou model female! my undaunted muse!
"Go on and write! for what have you to lose,
E'er had, or will have? tell them what you think!"
She cries each day, all day; "why should you shrink!"

What humbug choose? so many are the sorts!
"See! on the Fine Arts, what enormous warts!
These fungi nigh their beauteous forms conceal—
Respond first to their piteous appeal!"

Our country has no kings whose arms can hold,
The artist when in death his heart grows cold;
(Why must an ill to good be ever nigh—
The first removed, the other too must die)

Yet artists must die somewhere, that is sure—
Well, let them perish as do all the poor!
Here, merit 's measured by the rule of cash,
What fails in this, is deemed but worthless trash.
When men of mark, the highest in the land,
The *names* of Fine Arts do not understand,
Their devotees may look for naught but scorn,
To be poor devils always and forlorn.
Read JEFFERSON, philosopher and sage,
Who stamped his views on his and our own age—
Read Jefferson, the liberal advocate
Of science, learning, freedom in the state,
Tells young men, traveling, they need not go
To galleries of Art in Europe, no;
The useful, profitable, they must learn,
Their country's gratitude and love to earn! (13)
Yet there are men who will defy the tide,
The time, the world, the evil powers beside;
Thus mulish, for posterity would carve
A name, and long before 'tis finished, starve;
But Genius, such as ne'er was known before,
Now its transcendent light on us doth pour.
Who to the power-man, T. D. Bones, Esquire,
Sculptor, or BILLEM SORRY, can aspire!
Of their great deeds the last himself shall tell,
My only care that I repórt him well.

Billem Sorry, Esq., after announcing his supereminent and entire ability, delivers an oration on the history of Art in Cincinnati and the West, at the inauguration of the Pioneer Monument, executed by Tremendous Dead Bones, Esq., Sculptor. The oration being faithfully reported by the author. (14)

"Friends! fellow-citizens! I greet ye all!
Me have ye chosen, I obey your call,

To utter what lies latent in each heart—
Love, admiration, for all beauteous Art!
Well have ye chosen; *I*, *I*, am The Man,
The only man who such vast themes can span!
Ah, happy chance! for seldom are combined
The great occasion and the greater mind!
Assembled are we in a solemn state,
A work of Genius to inaugurate;
An honor to ourselves, our sires, our land!
It will the wonder of the world command!
When I have done, yon vail we will withdraw,
Then will you be entranced with joyous awe!
Then see sublime ideas to stone congealed—
In shapes of beauty to your eyes revealed—
All from the teeming brain of T. D. Bones,
Esquire, Sculptor; then, then, in thunder-tones,
Your voices will approve his master-mind,
That leaves all others, barring mine, behind!

"With forests clothed, dark, dusky lies the land;
The almost unpierced gloom, how solemn, grand!
A prairie here and there peeps at the sun,
And holds up flowers for him to shine upon;
Seldom disturbed, what silence! eloquent!
Yet guarding secrets to its keeping lent—
Whose mounds, whose walls of earth, of stone,
Whereon those trees ten hundred years have grown?
No letters, hieroglyphics, giving date,
No names of nations, builders, nor their fate!
One fact from their construction do we know—
Man wars with man forever here below.
The Indian follows, how? when? tell who can!
O'er *him*, now lowering, looms *his* fated ban!
For see! another peers with calm, *pale* face—
There mark dominion's deep, determined trace!

There mark the hatred gleaming in his eye,
Eager to close the Red Man's destiny!
His heritage the Indian strove in vain,
Strove with spasmodic fierceness to retain;
Too savage he, a civil knave to make—
His sullen spirit slavery scorned to take—
Since he could not be used, why should he live?
A needless question, which I pray forgive.
Restless, relentless and resistless, soon,
A People followed the adventurous Boone.
Insatiate, some say, was their lust of land—
Why should they not the Continent demand?
Men are but brutes with larger, firmer brain—
The strongest ever sovereignty attain;
It is our pride that we from sires descend,
Whose prowess conquered what it could defend.
But who the tale heroic has not heard,
Of men and women who their danger shared?
I told it to you at our festive board,
When on my wings, sustained, sublime, I soared,
So far, to such unprecedented heights,
That none could follow my exalted flights!
Therefore, to-day, our history of Art,
Shall be my speech, to future times a chart.
How glows my soul with this grand, glorious theme!
What facts! more splendid than the wildest dream!
How swells my pride at such a wondrous land!
Yestern a wilderness where now I stand!
How soon a gloomy forest-continent
Doth culminate in this great Monument!
Queen City of the West! high, sovereign name—
Known in thy youth to much artistic fame!
Then wert thou, but a score of years agone,
A beauteous princess on her sylvan throne,
While lofty hills, with treasures filled and crowned,
Of stone and wood, obedient, stood around;

Thy diadem, a dome of purest blue,
Made brilliant, while it blended every hue;
No dark and dingy smoke, no greasy soot,
Then tarnished colors and defiled with smut;
'*La belle rivière*,' sheen with the sun's bright beams,
Welcomed dark Licking, Makatewa's streams;
Wild flowers and fruit to maidens and to boys,
Occasion furnished for hilarious joys—
A pastoral city may I call it, where
Much mental culture breathed sweet country air,
No squalid poverty shocked sight and sense,
And cheerful labor gained its recompense.
Here, intellect, removed from hampering rules,
Transmitted stupidness and modern fools,
Could its original ideas test,
Discard authority for what is best;
New principles of life were thence evolved,
And practice, doubt to certainty resolved.
Our rich NICK LITTLEWORTH in Art thus founds,
A rule that to his shrewdness much redounds;
I quote his words; they are by far the best,
Though in a somewhat homely phrase exprest—
'Give artists work!' he cries, 'I'm no such fool!
G—d d—n 'em, starve 'em! starve 'em! that's my rule!
To bring them out, it is the only way,
The shiftless, good-for-nothing dogs, I say!'
How brightly Littleworth's example shines!
How well with practice he his words combines!
Consistency—a virtue very rare—
In this, is surely his beyond compare!
His house will not all through, above, below,
Two thousand dollars worth of Fine Arts show! (15)
Pictures, he says, he buys at auction, low;
What business tact! on this he builds his fame,
An honor makes of what should be a shame!

Wide as the land his name as Patron rings,
And READ, mellifluent, his praises sings! (16)
Yet Littleworth *this* sum e'en deems too much,
For though to gold all things turn at his touch,
Yet in the poor-house doth he fear to die—
Starvation dreads *he* as *his* destiny!
To be thus forced to eat of his own dish!
Worse to mine enemy I could not wish!
And I would grimly joy to know that fate
Avenges better far than bitterest hate!

"'G—d d—n 'em, starve 'em!' this is curt and new;
Who fails to recognize its cheapness too?
And *I* a novel principle proclaim,
Entitling *me* to everlasting fame—
That Genius need not labor to achieve
The greatest ends, who ever would believe,
Till I, in law, prove my transcendent power—
Till Bones and CHURCH to Art give their rich dower—
The world stands wondering at Aurora Leigh,
To brilliant BROWNING bends the knowing knee! (17)
'T is by the grace of God our deeds are done;
We prove by them that we all labor shun.

"Not so did they of whom you now shall know—
Our pioneers in Art, a goodly show.
They diligently Nature sought to find,
To whom she proved a mistress not unkind;
If one can not create, it is confest,
To copy closely, is by far the best.
Amongst the painters CORWINE must be named, (18)
For faithful likenesses so justly famed;
Too raw the country, and his death too soon,
To bring his talent to a brilliant noon.
And MORGAN, rising higher, never knew (19)
His greatest scope, for he died early too.

I knew him; let me pause a moment here,
And to his memory give a kindly tear;
A princely fellow, who could do and dare,
Soon struck, I know not why, with blasting care.
Thou reachest all, thou most malignant power—
None, none, escape thy secret, certain hour!
There are still others who have been asleep
Or long or not, for whom none care to weep.

"I turn and welcome those who live, to verse,
With meaning pregnant and construction terse.

"What shall I say of JAS. H. BEARD and T. B. Read? (20
Their early pictures do no praises need;
As painters—pigmies, great although they are,
Since their achievements in the Art of war!
When rebels threat the Queen of all the West (21)
With ravishment, and thus disturb her rest,
Among her many mighty men of Mars,
None made of her defense less of a farce—
For Bacchus lent them his efficient aid,
Of all her heroes made none less afraid;
Captains they were, and steadied at their posts,
If not themselves, perhaps the warrior hosts!

"There are yet other names: the FRANKENSTEINS,
(The Lord forgive the eldest all his sins)
Though both to Nature's imitation slaves,
The elder, precedent, opinion, braves,
Declares that we with open eyes can see,
Is but a stupid, childish fallacy;
He's mad; of late has ta'en a fit to fight,
And means a most satiric piece to write.
Let not my justice, gallantry and wit,
A LILLY MARTIN SPENCER here omit; (22)

The humor of the lower life she shows,
Wherein but few superiors she knows.
ALONZO DOUGLASS! wisely hast thou done, (23)
A pinched existence and the Arts to shun;
In thy vocation, none surpass thy skill—
This proves thy power to paint, if such thy will.
BRANNAN hath labored with the brush and pen; (24)
When first he wrote, he satirized some men,
Who in their hats would "carry bricks" he said—
They, from this demon, drink, long since have fled—
But Brannon! ay, how will this world turn round!
With red-hot bricks doth *his* hat now abound!

"WILLIAM H. POWELL is the only one, (25)
By whom my head in paint was ever 'done';
He had the sense to see its noble lines!
To see its beauty with such strength combines!
Ohio's Legislature boasted then
My membership; all who are present ken
I made a most extraordinary speech—
Then Powell paints me—my sublimest reach!
As moves athwart the burning mountain's brow
The black and belching smoke, my anger now
Moves o'er my frowning front, a dun, dark glow—
Beneath and through this beetling monster-mass,
Like disemboweled flames of earth, now pass,
Flash fiercely forth, forked lightnings from mine eyes—
Sulphureous vapor from my nostrils flies,
As does from Death's, when he the Pale Horse rides;
While, like the lava down the mountain-sides,
My eloquence o'er all my hearers rolls,
And burns conviction to their very souls!
Thus Powell painted me; I sat perforce,
He charged me nothing—that was quite of course;
But Billy's little bill I undertook
Should pass the Legislature, hook by crook;

This was, to paint a picture for the State—
I got it through; but we had fierce debate.

"HIRAM POWERS' plastic portraiture demands, (26)
The highest tribute from impartial hands.
His figures called ideal are not such—
Of Nature imitated show too much;
And yet too little Nature do we find
To satisfy the realistic mind.
The Greek Slave? No, I can not call it good,
Although I wish with all my heart I could.
"And CLEVENGER, thy name adorn my speech, (27)
Nathless the highest thou didst never reach.
And, JOHN L. WHETSTONE, thou, mine ancient friend, (28)
Who didst begin well nigh where others end,
And who, like Douglass, shunned artistic woes,
Thy name shall bring this record to a close.

"Art breeds some people of a curious kind—
Their character is not with ease defined:
Ridiculous—pestiferous—will do—
Ye critics, amateurs, I mean you, you!
Thee! leanest, lankest, longest of the tribe,
Thee! BILLY 'DAMS, I glut to jeer and gibe!
Before our most high court that painted thing,
Thou call'st a landscape for its trial bring;
Who sees such forms, such tints upon this earth—
Thy barrenness fore'er repeats this birth!
To our Art-union dost thou sell this daub?
To do so is no better than to rob! (29)
To rob? ay, scoundrel! in a twofold way:
No artist, the Art-union laws did say,
Should be an officer thereof, to sell
To it his works—the meaning 's plain and well;
Thou held'st an office there; thus, at that time,
To sell thy daub to it was double crime!

Thou wert no artist—but an amateur?
Bold villain! dost thou bring excuse so poor?
But MUSSEY proved all this in the Gazette—
Thou hast not dared to contradict it yet.
Thy body is the picture of thy soul!
All wrinkled, shriveled, thinned into a pole;
'T is printed plain on thy disfigured face,
What made it so, 's humanity's disgrace;
An old man, withered by his vices—what?
It is thy *character* and not a blot!
I know that Daniel Webster, Henry Clay,
Could drink and gamble and do worse, they say;
It made their work, their life, more human, broad—
They served and were exempted by their God!
But thou art nothing but a wreck of vice;
Thy *work* is fuddling and to fondle dice.
Is this to live? yes, gamble and get drunk,
That men may shun thee as they do a skunk—
And wretch! thy patriotism nobly shows!
Into the street for rent unpaid it throws
An absent soldier's family; the wife,
Of one, who guards with his thy worthless life—
A foul-mouthed monarchist with mumping chops
Mumbling: 'The People are but rabble' tops
Thy physical, thy moral, mental stench!
What! callous yet! and wilt thou never blench?
Is there no spot where shamelessness may feel!
All putrid skin! none quick to my barbed steel?

"There 's still another who deserves a niche;
A busy woman, but a venomous——— (30)
Her tongue has placed her far outside that pale,
That female weakness, men will not assail.
To reach the upper-ten how she will scheme—
'T is hard to rise on medicated steam!

If she at last a surly sufferance gains,
Her cringing low a dubious place obtains.
Her artful artlessness is wondrous skill,
Her artless artfulness more wondrous still.
Some think her character without a taint,
While others know a sinner, not a saint.
She now, since age has laid her on the shelf,
In chastened Magdalens concerns herself,
And brings to light, from marble, human shape,
As skillfully as monkeys men can ape;
Her body 's changed to grossness and her mind,
In correspondence does not lag behind.
Who is this unadulterate dunghill dame?
Nay, nay, enough; I will not tell her name.

"A nonesuch peers and proves a happier theme;
See o'er his face sweet self-complacence stream!
A handsome man, a gifted connoisseur—
His knowledge comes by Nature he is sure!
He says it is not study—that 's all fudge—
A gift enables him of Art to judge!
Friend KARRMANN also heads that knowing class, (31)
Who all but foreign daubs as worthless pass,
Then purchase only when the name is great—
Then hear them proudly and profoundly prate!
Calame has crazed KARRMANN and ANDY BURT, (32)
While both leave merit here without a shirt.
'T is true, they know no better, do their best;
But that I'll also say of all the rest.

"Poor, punning PEYTON SYMMES I will not blame; (33)
And if a comma could his wrath inflame,
His genial nature pleaded for the pest.
How he was wont to haunt that artists' nest,
Famous Foote's Row, of yore their favorite seat,
And others who their rent could never meet;

For FOOTE was easy, generous, and rich,
And let them pay or not, no matter which.

"I love to praise my kind whene'er I can—
I love to say he is or was a man!
SAMUEL E. FOOTE I venture to record (34)
As one who found acceptance with the Lord.
With him, his kindness did not pass away—
Some can remember if they can not pay.
No youthful energies by him were crushed,
No cheeks with helpless indignation flushed,
Because a business man must have his dues—
But when another stepped into his shoes,
His fostering Row of Art, of Physic, Law—
Ah! when the greedy GRIFFON struck his paw
Into the marrow of its hapless set,
And clutched the little money they could get—
When Foote must sell and Griffon bought, alas!
Their doom was fixed; whom would not he harass,
Who for vile lucre did not spare his blood—
Just indignation! whelm him in thy flood!
A man whose sphere chills with Siberian cold,
Whose charity is show, whose love is gold,
And gluttony, where he his fill can feast—
Thus one with method makes himself a beast,
Another rises to the gods above,
And both do nothing but what best they love.

"Next STETSON, of Art-union frauds the prince, (35)
Reduced to poverty and feeling since.
Art-union, bank, both to perdition went,
Of which he was the skillful president.
What harm, if widows, orphans, were made poor,
His shares were few, his wealth still all secure;
At last fatuity *his* money lost—
For wanting more, mid breakers *he* was tost;

Of all his work 't is *the* surprising thing—
Nor do I grieve that I can have this fling!
This Stetson here, and WETMORE in New York, (36)
Art-unions used for vile and villainous work;
The People freely paid, true Art to speed,
But in its name would not corruption feed;
The growing popularity of Art,
These rascals stifled at its very start.

"Academies of Art were born and died;
To rear one in our midst, all skill defied; (37)
The strongest-lived by ladies was conceived,
That *they* miscarried can it be believed?
Yet proved it an abortion like the rest,
And all because 't was born without being drest.
It may be well to show how this was done,
That future times the like mishap may shun.
Nick Littleworth's new rule was followed much;
Drawbacks it had—the case is ever such.
Without th' Antique and the old Masters' aid,
No artists, fit for aught, can now be made;
But how can they this far-off fountain reach,
When we do practice more than e'en we preach,
This 'starve 'em!' how to go, e'en if they would?
In this dilemma long the subject stood—
The horns of a dilemma to divert,
The ladies are proverbially expert—
'We'll bring th' Antique and the old Masters *here;*
Not the originals, if they 're too dear—
But perfect copies that for such will pass.'
They promptly moved, collected cash, *en masse,*
Sent Mrs. E. to Europe for the rest. (38)
When she returned, she brought—but oh, ye blest!
'What! these indecent, naked fellows, Gods!
These trulls are Goddesses? who were the clods,

When did they live, who made these nasty things!'
Thus, thus each woman horror shriller rings!
One big, big, fat one, throws aloft both hands,
Exuding sweets from all her pores she stands,
Convulsed she gasps, she chokes, she can not speak—
And though her terror other outlets seek,
Too great the shock, her forces must knock under—
Her bosom's billows almost burst asunder,
With short—still shorter—shorter—jerks—they heave,
Till whew! with one long shriek all sense takes leave,
She faints, she plumps upon the dirty floor,
And though some loose her stays behind, before,
They crowd around and stifle her still more;
The broad and bulky bosom is laid bare—
Ah! what a shocking, sickening sight is there!
Some things will happen, why, God only knows—
Must fate mock modesty in her dread throes?
Alas! alas! but that 's the way it goes!
Bosom exposed, and farther down in front—
What shall I say that will not be too blunt—
Flat on her back, her hoops throw up an arch,
Through which a legion of lewd loves could march;
Monstrous mishap mock-modesty befell,
To spare not e'en its very citadel!
"These sights and sounds combine as rare a treat,
As miserable mortals here may meet:
Outlandish e'en mid this odd scene, this din,
Yon maid of years—unspecked by soil or sin—
Stares silent, long, with mouth and eyes—'what's this—'
She says at last, 'here's something quite amiss!
It is unnatural I know, I'm sure!
I never saw—my memory is not poor—
I never saw the like in my born days!'
Her neighbor listens, stares at *her* and says:
'Poor thing! you have no husband yet to know,
That that is right and just exactly so.

These *statutes* show the men are not like us,
And that's the reason we make all this fuss!'
The joke is good, too good indeed to keep,
And so it quickly through the crowd doth creep;
The uproar lulls, a titter runs around,
And then the walls with laughter loud resound!
The maiden stares still more, her face abashed,
Is yet with angry, questioning doubting dashed—
She finds she is the focus of all eyes—
Their wicked looks infuriate—she cries:
'I *am* like other people—just like you!
I wish to God those curious shapes were true,
And I could be just like them! then you'd see,
How I would serve you if you came near me!'
Her crinoline a circle now describes,
Then backward flies a tangent at their gibes,
Goes through the door at a terrific rate,
And leaves the others to deliberate.
Deliberate! there was much pro and con;
While some insisted to put breeches on,
The liberals favored Adam's simple dress—
The savage sneered: you could not well have less!
The music-motions of a lady's tongue,
Are not perpetual, as has been sung:
The liberals for the fig-leaf gained the day,
And a committee is now on its way,
That Mr. Fazzi may amend th' Antique, (39)
And mitigate the grossness of the Greek!
'Ah, Mr. Fazzi! those—those—casts—you know—
We want them covered with a fig-leaf, so — — —'
And there they halted—' What! what! how is that?
You want all over covered and for what?'
'Oh, not all over, Mr. Faz—' 'Then where?'
'Oh, what a simpleton he is! why *there!*'
Directed by a desperate parasol,
He comprehends at last—' oh, that is all?

I will do anything for you Madame—
What curious peoples ! oh, what fools ! oh d—n !'
He put leaves on ; and though he chuckled much,
Swore more while giving his completing touch.
"At the Mechanics' Institute these casts now are ;
The fighting Gladiator's quivering buttocks, bare,
With all appurtenances dependent there,
Are quite conspicuous from the street below—
Trouble begun once none the end can know—
This stumbling-block will rise up still I find—
Come, Mr. Fazzi, fig-leaves for behind !

"Here brightly shines our Little Nick again ;
In chastity a leader among men,
From Powers' Greek Slave he turned with great disgust—
The marble figure, nude, created lust !
"Such things the ladies from abroad then brought,
That without pay our artists here be taught ?
How frequently are good intentions foiled,
And great things by the mean and petty spoiled '
The ladies from the very first somehow,
With these poor artists got into a row—
They slapped their free door in the artists' faces—
Of course with all appropriate grimaces—
They cried : 'You shan't get in, if you don't pay !'
And so these artists stay out to this day,
And have not learnt a thing in Art they say.

" 'T was my intention to contrast the Real—
The lesser with the greater Art, th' Ideal—
And Genius prove another word for fate,
That needs not industry to make it great—
'Twas my intent to show I do not work—
That I ne'er study where the gist may lurk—
The rules of evidence—all—all—despise,
For which some lawyers will read out their eyes—

That in no case my cases I prepare—
My Genius trust the jury to o'erbear—
But it is late and I must stay my speech,
Just when the grandest sentences I reach.
I never do get done; it is my fate,
To be unfinished and forever late;
I do not doubt but thus I shall miss heaven
When sounds the latest trumpet and be driven
To seek salvation with a generous devil,
Whose realm all comers enter without cavil—
"Remove the vail! Bones! from thy awful height,
Blaze! blaze! through time thy brilliant beacon light!"

As this mighty creation of the arboresque and statuesque order is unvailed to the thousands watching with eager eyes, they burst into a shout that shakes the earth; the cannon booms; Mr. Phlipps *surveys* it, falls down and worships!

PART II.

THE AUTHOR ONCE MORE SPEAKS FOR HIMSELF.

SEE! yonder Billem Sorry strides ahead!
In front of th' age his long legs make his tread!
And yet he fails like me, like all I find,
Of just appreciation from his kind.
Some get too little; many far too much—
How eagerly all at the phantom clutch!
Yet are we all, whatever we may seem,
Great, greater, greatest in our own esteem;
A strengthening plaster, efficacious, this,
For all the promises of life we miss.

Ere I this city leave for larger game,
For greater humbugs though not greater shame,
I have some other withering words to speak;
For once, forever, will I not be meek!
Who are these men whose humors I must take?
What fellows they, whose frown should make me quake?
I love to love; but I love too, to hate!
Because they're rich my case I must not state?
For any cause be silent while they prate?
I must still stand while still my cheeks they smite?
By heaven! I'll turn and to the death I'll fight!

I've long been ravenous as a famished bear—
I've waited, watched, and worked till I could tear!
With gentle pats I'll paw the thing I like—
With hungry hate the hated thing I'll strike!

Once more that ragged, dirty little man,
That son of squat St. Crispin I must scan, (41)
A farewell word to Littleworth must give,
A word in season since we both still live.
He knows the crooked ways much to possess,
Pure, precious grapes to poisonous wine can press,
And make some scribblers whom he soaks with drink,
A benefactor blaze him at his wink. (42)
How vast are not his views! to turn a penny,
His combinations equal are to any;
He first gets Dr. Mackay steeped enough, (43)
In th' Illustrated London News this stuff
In the most choice of thundering terms to puff:
Then Nick packs up some of this vinous ware,
Sends—how that deep-dyed Democrat will swear—
Sends it to GEORGE M. DALLAS, Minister, (44)
From all these great United States, to her
August, puissant, Majesty Brittanic—
" He might as well take me for a mechanic!
What! make me a commission merchant, ME,
Minister Plenipotentiary!"
Cries Dallas, while his eyes pop from their sockets:—
"*I* take these bottles with me in my pockets—
Thus to state-dinners of these nobles go—
When asked to wine, pull out my bottle—oh—
May 't please your Grace, first take with me a swig—
By G—d! as soon dance then and there a jig!
I am to serve these nobles with his wine—
I tell them when they come with me to dine,
That orders sent to Cincinnati, O.,
Will be filled forthwith with punctilio—

My Lord! my little per centage then, you know— —
With all the twists of trade I am to trick 'em— — —
Were he but here! out-doors my man should kick him!
But first, by heaven! I do believe I 'd lick him!!"
And stately Dallas his fierce anger churns,
Lifting his loftiness this thing he spurns:—
Did Dignity e'er suffer such mayhem?
And *Democratic* Dallas is its gem— — —
Our Littleworth here failed to gain his aim;
But all great men sometimes have done the same,
With us it did not dim his fulgent fame—
Large anecdotes they still give of his wit,
And we still laugh because there 's not a bit;
He is so queer, original, they cry,
And cite as proof his curious charity:
He helps but those whom no one else relieves,
The God-and-man-abandoned whores and thieves? (45)
I know not who it is such stuff believes;
If this helps any one it helps himself,
It is a cunning trick to keep his pelf,
If he some Cyprians succor in great straits,
Some conscience haply still his soul berates—
They call it charity, a novel touch
To help the poor things when he 's made them such!
What tales obscene habitually he tells,
That prove whereon his nature fondly dwells;
For Art, for all the subjects termed refined,
Here have we then a pure, ingenuous mind!
Say not that I assault an imbecile,
A crazed old man; do not to me appeal
To stay my hand from one who 's near his goal—
Did *he*, when *I* was helpless, d — n his soul?
Did *he*, a man of fifty then (a time
When passion 's calm, and judgment in its prime),
Did he attack a poor, nigh friendless boy,
Did he pursue him with malignant joy

To crush him, all these years, or did he not?
I had no voice till now when near his rot—
Now, scorn and study both have loosed my tongue,
By none so well his requiem can be sung!
I hope he has enough sense left to read,
And feel how his blind malice bears him seed;
Th' advantage 's with him yet! his course is run;
His hate reached me when mine was but begun;
(I know no cause; he 's full of quirks and kinks—
It does not matter—I 'll not trace their links)
I do not know that he has hurt me much—
I doubt the fact—not that his will was such.
Why from my wrath this fellow then exempt?
And yet I can dismiss him with contempt.

Ha! does he die ere this is put in print? (46)
The devil take it, for the devil 's in 't,
Perhaps the one I wanted most to whip,
As I would swoop him up, gives me the slip;
There must be future life! see! at me still!
The grave abates not his malignant will!
A member of the bar in former days,
His death adjourns the court—my case delays—
Victorious to the end! for he knows well,
That I will never follow him to hell.

My rusty hat I pull o'er all I know;
Into a pocket thrust each hand and go;
The solitude I love, leave now and then
To learn the little ways of little men:—
Go to the street and at their doings look—
Bent earthward, how they sweat and swear and crook!
I gaze aloft! there all is still and broad—
Then feel as if perhaps there was a God.
I can not stop this further to define—
Come! to the north-east corner, Fifth and Vine:

Dry goods to sell that lucky corner pays;
There precious pranks now PRETTY POPKINS plays!
Poor fellow! riches turn the brain he has,
And make him quite forget what once he was.
It is but little more than fifteen years—
Ay! since a woman came to me in tears,
In widow's weeds, and told a harrowing tale;
I was romantic, young; *she*, poor and pale—
Her husband's daubs I promised to complete,
That starving children might be glad and eat;
A wicked man had done her wrong, she said—
I snubbed the man and risked a broken head.
This Popkins is her son, grown rich and rude,
Ripe, though not ready, for my scornful mood;
He recks not, rough to ride o'er me and mine—
(Ah, Popkins! wilt thou always feel so fine?)
Assuming, overbearing, insincere,
This hypocrite a Patron would appear!
For Art his cunning doth grand schemes devise,
All specious and all meant to blind our eyes;
Public proposals to the Scratch-club sends,
That he well knows e'en there will find no friends—

From earth to heaven! man's spirit spans the whole!
Yet small the space that sometimes holds his soul!
All things are God's; from low to lower Muse,
The lower still to sing do not refuse;
There is a bug—the bed-bug—loathsome thing!
How little! yet with poisonous stink and sting!
A shuddering horror feel it o'er you creep—
From out your clothes, your skin, your life you'd leap—
Give gold and fame, and woman, wine and wit—
Give anything but to get rid of it—
Thus Popkins' peevish pettiness annoyed,
And for a little while my calm alloyed.

Turn where you will, stupid presumption reigns,
And ill-bred ignorance scant sense enchains.
The Young Men's Mercantile Association,
The Library, affords an illustration:
Where have you put that bust of JOHN McLEAN? (47)
Emasculated are you ere you 're men?
I do not ask *why* to some hole 't was moved:
The fact your moral cowardice has proved;
Some potent idiot its truth reviles—
Your silly sycophancy bows and smiles—
When a malicious meddler says you must,
That burly thing by Bones supplants a bust,
That looks a man and by a man was made!
Of what you are and know, this gives the grade—
Fit for such fools are mud heads by a Bones!
I greet you, youngsters, three times three, with groans!

(Come, will you hire me to deliver this,
Since I appreciate your auspices?)

Some more sweet samples since my hand is in:
A half-made-up, a kind of sooterkin,
A stagnant, sloppy sort of thick and thin,
A Next-to-Nothing now my numbers nudge:
It poetry and paint presumes to judge:
It uninvited came into my den,
And damned, because I was not present then,
My dumb, deserted and defenseless daubs:—
The breech of this poor sneak Correction cobs.
I wrote the facts in detail at the time,
Th' ex-captain's character and looks in rhyme;
Some publisher can have it very cheap:
I'll make the drawings—then this chap will sneap—
NORRIS R. NORTON, numskull and negation, (48)
Stick up to public view for admiration!

I have a life-long friend, a woman too;
I painted her when still our years were few;
The picture showed the head, neck, hands, and arms,
The dress revealed, yet covered, other charms.
This souvenir regards she not a whit,
The latest fashion or a frame to fit;
She cuts the head and neck out, oval shape,
(That seems the fashion now her whim would ape)
The rest is rubbish; I look on and smile:
Obtuseness so profound must wrath beguile.
This is no isolated case; it is not rare,
But always found 'mong those we call The Fair.

Thus Vandalism treads into a waste
The whole domain of cultivated taste.
Yet shall we wonder if abroad we find
An ignorant, conceited, ruthless mind,
When artists little work and little know
And thus the weeds that choke them help to grow—
When those who boast of Art with so much stress,
Are noted for the little they possess?
Where is THE BEAUTEOUS TRUTH to find a place,
When her own votaries are blind and base?
The SCRATCH-CLUB do you tell me I forget,
That guzzling, gormandizing, smutty set—
Whose president is Billy 'dams or Bones—
Whose artist-members almost all are drones—
Whose only merit, merit is to steal—
Whose clumsy thefts mean ignorance reveal—
For none of them the human form can draw—
They can abide The Beautiful? oh, pshaw!
In their foul air THE BEAUTEOUS TRUTH can grow?
My God! no! no! now and forever, NO!!

With facts like these agrees our groveling Press;
So low *its* level, could it well be less?

How changed from HAMMOND's bold, straightforward days! (49)
Did he have mole-like, shrinking, devious ways?
I cherish him who to a boy was kind,
But honor more his honest, manly mind;
How coursed through the Gazette his pungent pith!
A "cut-throat Calvinist," one RICHARD SMITH, (50)
(I quote Charles Hammond's words) now crab-like creeps
Low at the base of Hammond's lofty steeps.
POTTER, proprietor, supreme, profound, (51)
Sticks his Commercial in the muddy ground,
With HALSTEAD cattle works his treadmill round. (52)
Once HENRY REED was eloquent and right, (53)
Though but a meteor flashing through the night—
A night still growing darker every hour—
Increasing ever too in baneful power—
A night of dullness having still no end—
Which nothing seems to freshen or to mend—
Not when Rebellion rears its horrent face,
Is there a line above the commonplace.
'T is fit such papers humbugs praise in Art—
It is of their own character a part—
'T is fit their scribblers should the truth abuse—
It is to them quite strange, quite monstrous news;
That bad may still have worse, will gain assent:
As human bodies must their ordure vent,
So bodies social organs do require,
Whose functions in their nature are no higher;
'T is fit therefore, though all in dullness meet,
A traitorous Enquirer be the filthy sheet.
The refuse of mankind, its scurviest hogs,
Illiterate, scurrilous and drunken progs,
Envenomed with malignant spite still more,
The more they feel their state can not be low'r—
Their sloth can there beslubber and bespew,
The patient work of men who reach THE TRUE.

One moment—JAMES J. FARAN, WASH. M'LEAN— (54)
You've only felt the pricking of my pen.
In your Enquirer were my daubs abused—
You see how well I've been with that amused.
Here I had quit you; but the Public Wrong
You daily do, to pillory I long.
Now with a low-born and a lecherous leer,
At chastity of soldiers' wives you sneer;
Then to your daily walk of life appeal—
By Public Indignation struck, you reel,
You meanly skulk behind the man you hire;
Your daily walk! do you not kindle fire,
Hell's fire, with purchased, prostituted pen,
To help the devil blast man's hopes again?
Your daily walk! you do not drink, whore, gamble,
And therefore righteously you claim to amble?
Bold, barefaced, blustering scorn of Right and Sense,
Lies little, low, unscrupulous, immense,
A cowardly, a covert course, to blind
The weak, the ignorant, the trusting mind—
The villainous scum into a horde to band,
Still more to spread the riot in the land—
This is your daily walk, a hellish walk;
'T is this of which you with such unction talk;
To rebels tender, chicken-hearted, meek,
While with the Union soldiers' blood you reek;
Patient and law-abiding is The Right,
Forbearing still, when Law would have it smite,
Or you would tread the air in mortal fright.
Your daily walk 's to teach your sons your treason!
If their bad-blooded brains could e'er grow reason,
And then meet with your record in this strife,
Would they not hide in their own blood the knife,
Which you struck at the struggling nation's life!
If, ignorant, a noble woman marry
One of your brood; if she his brat should carry

Into this world, and *then* learn whence it sprung—
From treason execrated though unhung—
Who 's there to say, this woman be to blame
To dash brat's brains out ere it do the same?

Ay, I had quit you, but the Public Wrong,
Cried to impale you on a higher prong.
Could I but spit you where the world would see
Your carcasses through all eternity;
Where, should men's scorn your quivering flesh consume,
Your bones would blazon your unburied doom;
Your eyeless sockets gleam and glare within,
Your gumless teeth would hideously grin,
Still animate with your most monstrous sin!

I will believe this life an episode—
I will believe there is a blest abode—
I will believe the brave abide above—
I will believe that there we still can love—
I will believe if here I lose a friend—
There, there, my joy with him will have no end!
Ah, could I speak the tenderness I feel,
Could tell how softly it doth o'er me steal,
When to the stars my moistening eyes I strain,
There of my friends who 're gone a glimpse to gain!
Yet on those stars what natives may be found,
In prejudice and privilege fast bound,
Who 'll not to them, as foreigners, unbend,
Grudging, like men, the room they think they lend?

I am not old and yet almost alone,
I hardly hear a once familiar tone.
From my stern purpose let me turn aside,
But for one moment let me cease to chide,
That I may syllable the praise of some,
Whose friendship ceased but with the life to come;

That I may honor others living yet,
And show that kindness I would not forget.

Once RICHARD CRUMP, thy face was by me limned; (55)
I gaze and see the picture's eyes undimmed;
I see therein enthusiasm shine
Resembling what I always saw in thine;
I will not then these pictured orbs despise,
Since they bring back to me thy vivid eyes.
Of all the men of work I ever knew,
In any path of labor men pursue,
None were like thee with holy fire consumed,
None were like thee to disappointment doomed.
By thee, to paint, was deemed delight divine,
Yet must thou do far other work to—dine.
When dread despair with damning drink I drowned,
When I in God and man no refuge found,
Thy letters gave me places of sweet rest,
Relieved the torture that my soul compressed.
My friend beloved! since thou hast gone from hence,
I've known disgust, defiant and intense,
Despised despair, and working, battling strong,
Have burst at last into indignant song.
I had, oh God! so weary grown of paint!
I bound, released from some accursed restraint;
If thou wert here, thy faith in me would laud
The work I do, and my intent applaud.
The flesh no longer feels its need to die—
Now swells and soars my spirit, sweeps on high—
Then, softened, mournful, melts to melody,
Subdued and saddened, seeking still for thee!

JOHN LOCKE! his name lends luster to my page; (56)
Few are his equals as a man and sage;
For science subtle agencies he sought,
And matter to a resolution brought,

Yet never ceased to treat it as a whole—
He ne'er forgot, nor robbed it of its soul;
Nor while the what, the why, and how, he booked,
Did he neglect to learn how it all looked.
All works of Art with interest he viewed,
Nor shocked with criticism coarse and rude;
Nor did he run to feel if they were slick,
As was the way and test of Little Nick;
But at the proper distance sought to find,
Intent and silent, there the painter's mind.
A student all his life, he knew the cost—
If good—each touch a thought not to be lost.
His praise, if it was gained, was something worth,
Because 't was thoughtful observation's birth.
One of the brightest jewels in thy crest,
Queen City! though thou seem'st not so impressed;
A mind of the first magnitude, it moved
E'en here among the stars whose paths it proved;
It needed not death's intermeddling care,
Not robbing us on earth, to place it there!

And not the least among the many dead,
Robert T. Lytle sunlight on me shed. (57)
The People loved him as their advocate,
Whose words could crush aristocratic hate;
The People loved him for so large a heart,
That all the world could come and claim a part.
E'en party hate must in his presence melt,
And hate a hatred it no longer felt.
But of this name I cherish more than one;
I loved the father, and I love the son. (58)
The last with high-toned chivalry leads men,
Who fight to make their country one again;
Though of his wounds he scarcely yet is healed,
Once more the foremost is he on the field.

The dying moon rises slowly from its bed
As if 't were weary of the life it led;
Darksome and gloomy looms midnight's expansion,
Sad, somber shadow dims the Lytle mansion,
Mantled more darkly, moaning move the trees
Their bending branches to the blighting breeze;
And restless and uneasy is each leaf,
Chattering as if there was no other grief,
Save what each tells with such a mournful sound,
Or still aloft, or flickering o'er the ground;
Soughing in sorrow so, October wind,
Seeking, like me, communion now to find,
With loved and lofty spirits, once true men,
Whom we as mortals ne'er shall see again?
With reverence I bare and bow my head—
They may be near, the good, the gallant dead—
WILLIAM HAINES LYTLE! my friend's son, my friend,
How premature, yet glorious is your end!
I will not weep, though I am very sad—
I can not joy, and yet I should be glad—
How I have loved these rebels hitherto—
Shall I not love them more for killing you?
Without your blood these monsters were not sated—
Oh, I have learnt how much they must be hated!
What bound you so to me you did not know?
'T is very plain, quite plain why it was so—
When ANDREW JACKSON stood in yonder door,
On his way home, to battle thence no more,
I was a stripling in the foremost crowd,
'Gainst will and wont to push or to be loud:
Your father with impatience cleared a space,
But passed me by as I looked in his face:
He knew me not when afterward we met,
Or, if he did, he chose it to forget;
But I remember that sweet courtesy,

And that he always was most kind to me—
God bless him! generous to a fault was he!
This, this it was that bound you to me fast,
For I loved him and his—you, unsurpassed,
For kindness, courtesy and courage—nay,
Can I no longer keep these tears away—
Ah, it is hard to bear and must be borne—
And yet I should be glad—why must I mourn—
For you have died for that great cause that gives
His liberty to every man that lives!
The name of Lytle will be linked with those
For whom the righteous heart with ardor glows:
Our people feel you lost in your life's morn;
In Cincinnati, here, where you were born,
They thronged to bless you, sigh their last farewell,
As military pomp, funereal bell,
Buried their hero whom they loved so well!
'Twixt leaves still restless, 'gainst its sheen so darkling,
The now risen moon, see! like star-clusters sparkling!
So through earth's tremulous and midnight gloom,
You with the Glorious now our souls illume;
The diamond-stars eternal peer above—
The pearl-clouds come to life with light of love—
Brighter and greener grows the purple blue,
Like human nature when men rise like you—
Like him who was your noble father's guest
As he passed on to find his final rest—
Like Andrew Jackson—hail! all ye, ye Blest!

When in the grave the Union giants slumber,
Then slavery springs the free North's days to number;
When lived a Jackson, Webster and a Clay,
Was for rebellion no auspicious day.
Jackson! well traitors wait till he is dead—
They knew what he would do from what he said—

I but beheld his specter near the grave,
Yet still erect, still competent to save;
Jackson! what honor thronged erst round this name!
Now, now, alas, how great should be its shame!
Now its renown a *Stonewall* Jackson shares— (59)
STONEWALL! fit title that mad monster bears,
Who last the bandage from that ulcer tore,
That damnable, disgusting, running sore,
Thousands of years have not, not yet healed o'er—
That proneness of mankind to love the lash,
If but laid on them with a certain dash,
Complacently to lick then the gangrene,
Thinking the chronic sore they thus keep clean—
God! Christ! Religion! and Civilization!
Hear ye those shouts of ardent admiration,
For onslaughts on what *you* teach as the Right,
Because the villain does not fear to fight!
How well it works, this Christ-machinery
For hoisting into heavenly company—
In Right, in Wrong, how well are they not drilled,
When they lament this slavery's bloodhound killed!
E'en WHITTIER tells us we must drop a tear
Upon this stenchy Stonewall Jackson's bier,
Because he spared a fool, old Barbara,
While he was rushing on to—ha! ha! ha!
Only to rend his country, nothing more!
Dog-demon! pious! till his head is sore!
How he with Calvin-venom men inspires:
How he their brains, their hearts besotted, fires:
How he their blinded fury then impels
On their own country's love with hideous yells—
Hear how the fool-fiends bound with blasting breath—
They must be in at their own Freedom's death!
To be there first, how hotly Stonewall rides—
And can it be that God with such sin sides?

No! no! the evil giant soon is blown—
He rides to death—hosanna! 't is his own!
Tears! tears! ah, yes, tears I will freely shed,
But tears of unmixed joy that he is dead!
Call me ferocious in vindictiveness—
Pugh! pugh! there 's this pugnacious scoundrel less;
This unmatched executioner, he whom
Hell surely holds if hell for him had room;
Inscrutable, he ever lived at all,
Or since he did, with powder and with ball,
Rather than at the rope's-end he should fall!
  Look at the picture of his precious face:
There, not one line of nobleness you trace;
No, no; the truly noble are with us,
They must be—all the great, good, noble, generous.
In Europe, those who fear this nation's power,
Therefore of its division hope the hour,
And say so honestly, we may respect,
Although we think their fears are incorrect;
But those who, gluttonous of privilege,
Keep the herd brutes, make of their backs a bridge,
And then o'er life's morasses dry-shod stride—
Legions of liars, and of fools beside—
And, by the Lord, these do turn up in schools—
They trample on all decent, righteous rules—
They bellow, bluster, blunder, loud and long—
The world is old enough to know what's wrong—
Self-evident 's the justice of our cause,
Founded on Nature's clear, inherent laws;
Those who our cause's righteousness deny,
Can know but little, or they know they lie;
"Plain people," said our honest President,
Plain people need on this no argument.

  All heads, all hearts, clear, true, just, generous,
In this great contest must, must be with us;

They need not tell me therefore, HIRAM POWERS, (60)
You with your country are in these dread hours;
I love to hear it though and send you greeting—
Here, in OHIO, we just had a meeting:
The People, we, the mass, the common herd,
On our affairs, for they *are* ours, conferred:
You lived with us once; with delight you'll thrill,
When told how we expressed our sovereign will.
A fact significant here let me note:
Many, who seldom did before, now vote,
Now, since they hear the devil's lusty roar,
They gather at the polls, his friends to floor.
Not much we said; but paper-billets dropped,
By which the cause with fresh support we propped;
Who 'll now hope that we ever will consent
To these United States' dismemberment?
Do we not know how Italy was torn,
For many centuries ere we were born?
For Unity, have we not cheered her struggle—
Like gawks we 'll gape while ours from us they juggle?
We only read, write, cypher; that 's enough,
And we know well why we elect John Brough;
Let hatred jabber; let it slander sputter,
We know on which side of our bread is butter.

And so I greet you, Powers, with glad, glad tidings;
There have not been, there will not be, backslidings;
State-sovereignty I fear and hate—
But our OHIO is a glorious State!
Since that dog DOUGLAS, dead, and, I hope, damned,
Disinterested patriotism shammed,
Since the Missouri Compromise was broken,
Unfalteringly for FREEDOM it hath spoken.
To love the whole land—state-pride of that kind—
With such there is no special fault to find.

Ohio, to whom God gave such great beauty,
How handsomely its children do their duty!
Its gentle hills and vales methinks I see
Waving with living, joyful sympathy;
A quiet pride peep from those prairie nooks,
Rippling more swiftly all its streams and brooks,
Their eyes flash back to heaven more grateful looks;
The trees don a more gorgeous autumn gear,
Though thousand-thousand-tinted every year;
From its sweet river to its ocean-lake,
Nature inanimate I hear awake—
Through the vast forests is a murmur moving—
Each leaf and twig 's ambitious of approving,
And blessing spirits breathe a softening haze
O'er the peerless sun's unclouded blaze—
Oh, Hiram Powers! I do not envy you
Young Italy's soft winds and heaven so blue!
Here in Ohio too those busts you made,
Extraordinary, of the highest grade;
Who in primeval wilderness would seek
The power, the finish, of the ancient Greek?
And if from father Eckstein you obtained, (61)
What men in centuries have only gained—
Those simple rules without which Genius blunders:
(Born, bred 'mong Indians, you had made no wonders)
And if a stray cast showed the mystery,
From which what had been done your eyes could see,
Though requisite, what would have been all these,
If *you* had not been there their power to seize,
With giant-genius lift unto men's sight,
In wild woods, Sculpture to its utmost height?
Do let me thank you for those priceless treasures
That are to me among my greatest pleasures.
I 'm proud now of its touch, that master-hand,
As it my head's dimension gently spanned;

And as I sit here, undisturbed, alone,
I look back on the years from which we 've grown,
And since I 'm told, in classic Italy,
You spoke my name, that you remembered me,
I may remind you of your courtesy,
And Doctor Alban Goldsmith's too—both kind— (62)
He 's now in that land none here live and find—
How good he was I did not realize,
To sit for me, a boy who untaught tries
To make a bust, and for the first time too;
But I know now how it all was; and you
Quit your immortal work at his request,
To see a boy's beginning at the best;
Encouragement, direction too, to give,
That are remembered ever as I live.
Then Spurzheim was in vogue: examining my head, (63)
" Here 's not much veneration," laughingly you said:
Yet I revere the Doctor, you, as men,
Than whom, for pencil, chisel, or the pen,
Handsomer, higher, has not all the race;
My mud head of him fell down on its face,
And with a big French brandy bottle made a crash—
Had but the Doctor had, or you not needed, cash!
There was a glorious subject for your skill—
Nature ne'er made a finer and ne'er will!
Her best art 's rare; *your* art is rarer still:
I *must* ask why did you not make a bust
Of this most splendid head that now is dust—
With highest Nature highest Art entwine,
That years in thousands may not now combine.
 His picture gazes at me as I write:
I painted it three twelve-months past, not quite:
Then with his prime had fled his full, dark hair—
Some richly-tinted gray locks lingered there,
Encircling like a halo that grand dome,
Wherein a god might choose to make his home;

His beard, now full, was still more richly gray:
There every tint seemed lurking with its ray.
His eye calm, clear; his glowing color too,
The freshness all retained it ever knew.
Where moves the Hudson's great erratic will,
Where, distant 'gainst the sky lean the Kaatskill,
Behold the Doctor standing on his lawn—
The form to fit the scene we now look on!
Behold the Doctor! Gotham's fashion-gear,
He 's doffed for something comfortable here;
While on the boat he twits me 'bout my hat—
'T is my turn now: what in the world is that!
Drab-colored, steeple-crowned, one side caved in—
Is that to any mortal hat akin?
A gray-blue jacket of knit wool, his form
To just below the hips fits snug to warm;
Of breeches thence you but a little see,
For soon looms up his boots' immensity—
Up, up, his thighs they come—I have seen none
Like them, since this enormous war begun;
Yet is this costume but another phase,
Wherein his nature dignity displays.
A farmer-neighbor talks to him who 'll say
(Most delicately courteous is the way):
"The Doctor knows," not you know, Doctor—thus,
To him these neighbors are all courteous.
Since e'en his bitterest enemy 's forgiven,
His smile benign seems like a beam from heaven.
A servant's little boy waits with a sled
Behind him, watching for his graceful tread;
The dog, a St. Bernard, no canine sham,
Quite ready to fall in is honest Sam.
Exultant vapors from the Hudson rise,
Mid these, like fairy land, its left bank lies,
And as they mount into the upper skies—

Are those their shadows on the Kaatskill's face,
That flit so blue, so fast each other chase?
The weeping willow's gold 's a roseate glow—
A thought of pink lies on the new-fall'n snow—
It is a morn with glories gushing o'er:
There, living, is my friend, kind as of yore—
Eve comes: out of the window as I gaze,
Exhaustless Nature wears another phase:
Eve comes: I look as I still wash my brushes;
High on the Kaatskill virgin snow yet blushes:
The scene is full of a mysterious charm;
'T is early yet: work fails not on a farm:
The Doctor, lithe and humming all the while,
The boy behind, all booted in his style,
The sled, the dog, move on in single file:
Their forms fade fast—and now I lose their roaming
Around that point, dark, dim, in this deep gloaming—

Thus man, good, glorious, like a god may be:
God's name read backward—Dog—that too is he;
Allied to all the brutes, no dirtier dog,
Divinity, ay, decency doth clog.
'Twixt Barrytown and Gotham's puffed-up pride,
Three years since a one-horse power steamboat plied,
Stemming most awkwardly the Hudson's tide:
One Captain Anderson commanded her:
It would be hard to find a dirtier cur;
I can not now tell why: some future time,
I 'll give particulars and string in rhyme,
A lot of other human dogs I 've known,
Who scratched the dirt that in my face was blown;
Great Gotham peers in sight; I 've work *there* now;
(If my verse labors like this steaming scow,
Few readers reach New York with me I trow).

Oh, prophet Mansfield, statistician, say (64)
When Gotham to Porkopolis gives way—
Has it not come yet, Mansfield-fate-fixed day?
If smoke proves fire, the Western Queen will stand
First may be 'mong the cities of the land;
If human gasbags are of greatness measure,
The Western city has enormous treasure;
Yet are her heroes not as much renowned
As those who in great Gotham may be found;
Its geniuses in fame have higher rank,
Although their brains be just as much a blank;
Its papers say, there fat corruption feeds,
No place more mending of its morals needs:
I care not for all this; I love New York,
Its enterprise so vast, its solid work.

PART III.

BETWEEN two isles steal some Atlantic billows;
Each isle still NARROWS, yet the strangers pillows,
Till these at last, by gentle, amorous play,
Gain glorious room for a most glorious bay;
Then joyously they throw two arms far out,
And clasp Manhattan Island round about.
On these large, stalwart arms will soon be laid,
The world's great, free and liberalizing trade.
Stamboul is steep; poor Venice lies so low!
Can sunlight through the fumes of London flow?
No smoke will e'er begrime OUR CITY'S brow!
Manhattan wears the crown of cities now;
God made it fairy-like! so beautiful!
For once man is not all undutiful;
What God so bounteously blessed, man's taste
Still beautifies, adorns, while it must waste.
The Central Park, itself a city's site,
Cost much, much money, but the thing is right;
And how delightful it will be when time
Shall bring to planted forest-trees their prime!
Go to Fifth Avenue, there 's nothing mean;
Nothing to fret the eye, how clear! how clean!

If there I may not live, I still may walk,
And of its wealth and beauty write and talk.

The hour is for the throng too late, too soon;
Low lies behind me half the eastern moon,
Silent, deserted, sleeping are the streets,
And most of those who have them, 'tween their sheets;
Delicious, dreamy drowsiness descends,
The listless moonlight with like gaslight blends;
In those young, thriving trees a leaf may stir,
To love of love a low light whisperer;
The stillness seems to grow more still and still—
But is this all that now the air doth fill?
Nay, nay, yon obelisk, this public square,
Of WORTH, of MADISON, the names they bear,
Melt the GREAT PAST with the GREAT PRESENT CARE!
But clear, a little paler than the sky,
Looms—is it that—or farther still—or nigh—
Nay, 't is a huge mass of white marble reared,
That men for money may with cheer be cheered;
Call it a tavern, sneerer, if you choose,
By this hour glorified unto the Muse,
Fifth Avenue Hotel looms dim but light—
Looms like our Future, beautiful and bright—
Ah, may we build a pile for all mankind,
Where they the best of Freedom's cheer shall find,
Where justice is the coin which they must pay
For their accommodation while they stay,
Where, if they choose, they can be at their ease
And with politeness do just as they please.

There is a breadth about and in this town,
Expanding e'en the crime on which we frown.
We must respect the intellectual scale
That can so vastly in the moral fail.

If monstrous frauds the public purse assail
Yet works gigantic public wants supply,
Bring calm convenience, sweet security;
Millions of money generously are spent,
That for the public good are truly meant.
Clear Croton, brought o'er hill and dale to bless,
Completes, or can complete, the cleanliness.
The ruling spirit here's not all a fraud,
To rob its fellow-man, defy its God.
  We should not close our eyes when men act well;
On all the good they do I love to dwell;
And so I linger as Our City lies—
Panting with life, does it need wings to rise—
And rose it not, the eagle of the land,
In wrath, with talons ready, first at hand,
To clutch Rebellion rampant by the throat!
Its Union larum listening traitors smote—
Oh, execrable, thou, New York, they cried—
Fools! *it* would help the Nation to divide?
Come! walk down any, walk down Chatham street;
See, how the stars and stripes your vision greet!
On horses, vehicles thick driving by—
You see them in each human being's eye;
Walk farther—there the Park expands in light;
From all the house-tops, St. Paul's steepled height,
The Nation's banner waves the Nation's might.
Oh, I could clap my hands for very joy!
Delight thrills me that has no, no alloy!
See there! our emblem o'er the City Hall—
It is not now New York—'t is NATIONAL!
Look eastward! like a wall of flaming brain,
The Government and Freedom to sustain,
Bold, busy is the patriotic press—
There floats our flag in all its gloriousness!
Across the Park, look south, or north, or west,
With our bright banner still your eyes are blest;

And Broadway shows more stars than heaven displays—
Who 'll tell me we have fall'n on evil days!
Let him who every human thing reviles,
Mark Broadway now; far as you see, for miles,
By human feet is jammed each foot of ground,
The trees and posts with human forms abound,
And every window, up, up, to the eaves—
On eaves and roofs the sky a crowd relieves!
Hark! hear those shouts! and see the kerchiefs wave!
The valiant march, THE CAPITAL to save!
The Seventh Regiment moves to the front,
The first to fly to brave the battle's brunt!
The Great Republic's plain Democracy,
First fought for by its Aristocracy!
Oh, in what age, what country would you live,
Where man a brighter phase than this can give!

Mammon, whom Milton meanest spirit calls,
Here proves that gold not all his soul inthralls;
Praise him I must whom moralists knock down,
That from his pockets they may fill their own.
Civilization springs from love of wealth,
The last, if general, proves the former's health.
All human things have a mean, selfish side—
Can Mammon not display pure, splendid pride?
The Government he now supplies with gold,
That liberty to slavery be not sold.
Lucre needs no republic to be free,
E'en despots love it, grant it liberty;
The nabobs of New York shall live in story,
Their names be haloed in this struggle's glory.
And Gotham e'en in Art some praise deserves,
Of other cities precedence preserves,
Pays well, somehow gets those who paint the best
(Some good work thus secures among the rest)

Its many Mayors and Governors of the State,
On painted canvas to perpetuate.
  Ruskin argues that daubers must have brains;
Is their case bad, since he takes so much pains?
Two New York painters other claims present;
A FULTON's head the steamboat doth invent,
While MORSE to words the wings of lightning lent—
That they had brains, few now in question call,
Though neither ever learnt to paint at all. (65)
  DARLEY can draw, and PALMER mold so well, (66) (67)
That of their merits with delight I tell.
  I greet you, CHARLES L. ELLIOT, as of old; (68)
We ne'er each other chill with envy's cold;
If one does well, the other can admire,
Regard still rising as he rises higher;
Ay, both of us can pity with a smile,
Men charging envy in the threadbare style,
To be characteristic of our craft;
Its true sons seldom use that small fry's shaft.
I learn, like me, you profit from the past—
To paint our best, we must not live too fast;
Besides the solid benefits this brings,
From little gnats it draws the little stings.

  A scratch-club's orgies once in Gotham roared, (69)
And Cincinnati's glories herein floored.
New York's Art-union miserably failed,
Fraud, favoritism, folly's fill entailed,
And unknown merit on its pales impaled.
That that man Wetmore, then its president,
When my Christ-pictures were for sale there sent,
Should scripture-pictures quite unpopular declare,
Or to dispute or to denounce I do not dare; (70)
For Christ himself became unpopular,
When he proved only the soul's caterer;

Now, Christ himself might be more popular,
Although he is our souls' great caterer;
I did not paint Christ-pictures any more—
On that part of the past I close the door,
And "shut the dog out," as Mrs. Browning says. (71)
But this is nothing—hear of JENNY LIND—
How this concern against her sadly sinned!
Its president, changed to one A. M. COZZENS,
(A goodly fellow, though such grow by dozens)
Shows Jenny Lind among the pictures round,
Exhibits a politeness most profound,
And what doth still more to his fame redound,
When Jenny *will* admire what he deems daubs,
His choice as *hers* upon the public fobs;
His likes of pictures as the *Swan's* rehearses,
And in *his* judgment Jenny Lind's reverses:
Like a true knight he seeks to save her credit—
So did he publish, so the public read it.
The architects of Gotham color show,
More than its daubers in harmonious glow,
In marble, brick, stone, slate and glass combine,
Tints that may hide defects in form and line.

Muse, forward! charge that stronghold! prove no hilding!
Storm, storm that New York Tenth Street Studio building! (72
An arduous task! for like to catacombs
Are all its darksome passages and rooms;
Forward! spring with a tiger's certain bound!
Charge! charge! hark! from those tombs what doleful sound!
Nay, WILLIAM HART through guarded lines goes free, (73)
His power to paint needs not a pass from me.
You are my prisoners, LEUTZE, you and PAGE— (74) (75)
On you I soon shall vent some special rage;
I can not now neglect, leave in the lurch,
Th' infallible, the true, the only CHURCH. (76)

Take care! touch gingerly! with kid-gloved hands—
So great a man the greatest care demands!
Can aught be said that can increase his fame?
May more notorious yet be made his name?
Can more be added to his many bays,
Whose work the people gaze at with amaze?
Poor NATIONAL ACAD'MY of Design! (77)
Its dingy shows fall into a decline,
While all rush into Church's like mad sheep,
To view his canvas-wonders vast and deep,
To see how he in paint can all outleap.
"Ah, exquisite! ah! did you ever, la!
The finest picture that I ever saw—
How beautiful! oh, do just look! I never!
See—how he made that water in the river—
That 's just my style! splendid! divine! oh dear!
That upstart Mrs. Smith! she, she, come here—
Nobody paints like Church the papers say— —"
So ladies chatter in their happy way;
Their time, if not themselves, they thus beguile,
For that indigenous, that furtive smile
Shows one another they note well meanwhile.
Perhaps men view the picture more, talk less,
Yet blindly praise with larger emptiness;
The women see *each other* clear at least—
The men see nothing at their very best;
What need Church care? for business 't is the same,
Since him THE GREATEST MASTER all proclaim;
Yes, all our papers say none paint like Church—
No, sir! go over all the world and search!

CHURCH'S NIAGARA! that classic phrase,
In Art conveys the very highest praise.
This picture must be moving, brilliant, grand,
To make so great a furor in the land!

Imperfect would be my Art-diatribe,
Church's Niagara not to describe.
Ere I do this it will me well behoove
To watch with care THE LORD'S NIAGARA move;
How in grand lines vast water-masses hurl,
In beauteous floweret-forms in detail curl—
Seem a huge crystal emerald cylinder—
Rolling as if no God their course could hinder—
How fields of darting foam-light fringe this green
With brilliant, yet most tender roseate sheen;
How giant spray-sprites drive with dripping dress,
Sweep high, flit low, with weird mysteriousness,
And how these weave a web of texture rare,
Sun-moon-loved Iris sisters to upbear — —
And how God's splendor seems inherent there—
For in the deepest gloom of darkest night
Still looms a lingering, lovely dream of light—
Where day and night forever soars the song
Of power, that knew not that it was so strong!

"And *do* you think that you can paint these Falls!"
O'er the din shrilly an old woman calls,
As trembling with a strange, exciting joy,
In painting them I all my force employ.
Why, what a fool you must be 's on my lips,
Why, what mad folly could my own eclipse,
If I did *not* think I could paint these Falls!
For months this view one half my day inthralls.
This is the key-note to the general talk;
Th' old lady, like most people, was a gawk;
They look at Nature, pictures, all the same,
And gabble most when they have greatest fame.
Sometimes an honest fellow comes along,
Not touched by any old, grandific song—
"This is Niagara!" with scornful leer,
"I don't see anything to look at here!"

Into a shapeless fool he will not bloat,
And prate sublime grandiloquence by rote.

Niagara moves fast; light, lightning faster;
Its thundrous voice still thunder owns a master;
Its blinding brilliancy, its gorgeous green,
Without the sun would it at all be seen?
Yet of all these, men in their petty way,
In colors and in words have much to say;
Then why should not Niagara be "done"
In words or paint, far better than the sun?
Man's imitations all are rather lame,
The best compared with Nature somewhat tame;
Ancients or moderns nothing ever wrote,
None painted, none the marble ever smote,
And gave the full, fresh Life we fear and feel and see—
The past, the future of the far eternity
In every object, moment, every thought—
All with that mystery so awful fraught— —
And that more dread uncertainty that moves
On with man's life—its constant shadow proves,
That something undefined from which man flies,
Yet longs to learn till his poor body dies—
That beasts seem conscious of—that follows all,
That man would drown in opium, alcohol,
In superstition's, folly's catalogue,
In anything that can his senses clog—
So, when man's best is done, mankind's great masses,
Can comprehend it like so many asses;
In its most perfect sense—this poor mankind—
Its precious eyes, it is the most purblind;
A lazy liar, leisurely, at ease,
Paints lies and proves the best man far to please.
The merit of good writing is more plain,
The masses herein greater breadth attain.

"And *do* you think that you can paint these Falls!"
In colors nor in words my spirit crawls—
A faithful picture patiently to give
I promise, may thy servant then still live?
Its pigment-painting proved an anxious thing—
'T will be less work Niagara to sing.

A limestone barrier of grand, mountainous lines,
Seeming unyielding, its main forms defines;
An isle, with many kinds of foliage crowned,
That may in temperate latitudes be found,
Shapes it to two unequal parts; besides,
An islet from the largest isle divides
The lesser from another, which we call
One, the American, one Center Fall—
The latter here is an affair quite small,
Though sixty feet wide and a very wonder
Of beauty, with a voice allied to thunder.
The rocky brink a sharp line marks across,
Seen through the waters as they o'er it toss.
These in their maddest mood and wildest storm
Must to this fundamental law conform.
How patiently they are avenging this!
For see! for miles extends a dread abyss—
They riddle, lick up subtly-tongued this rock,
Or at its shaly base defiance mock—
Mined by their spray 't is hurled to depths profound,
There by their feet to nothingness is ground.
All past and present data are agreed,
These great Falls ever southward thus recede,
Grow less and less in height, and so in time
Have lost already much of the sublime.
When many, many centuries ago,
These wondrous waters fell some miles below,
And when their width was narrowed to a third—
What movement then was seen, what roar then heard!

Perhaps then fifty feet deep were they heaped,
Ere finally three hundred down they leaped!
Could they be thus now for our poets' sake—
Then with what verses would the world they wake!
How much do we not lose in language grand,
Of great Jehovah and His hollow hand!
The greatest depth now on their convex brink,
Some twenty feet from thoughtless talk you'd think;
I judge 't is five; yet what majestic might,
One hundred sixty-six feet falls in height!
How huge this movement! how magnificent!
What splendor, gorgeousness are with it blent!
If in the cars from Chippewa you go,
Should suddenly the falling waters show
As you look down some fifty feet below,
You from your seat, as I, may startled spring—
My God! what's that! that moving, bright green thing!
May be your words of doubt, alarm, amaze,
When for the first time there you see it blaze.
Observe—of grandeur it has yet enough,
To make me vapor my sublimest stuff.

Near Church now go, on the Canadian shore,
(It is the left) close to the rush and roar.
The Horseshoe Fall, far greater of the two,
Almost encircling us, from here we view.
Its brink resembles three sides of a square,
Irregular, changed by the waters' wear;
The horseshoe shape being gone this will attest;
One side is facing east, one north, one west.
Near us, the waters' brink 's so near, it hides
The plunging waves on th' nearest of the sides;
Trace their brink's line up stream from near our feet—
There see it bulging out—again retreat—
From hence to that last point the waters rollick,
Bounce toward their plunge in a mad, dancing frolic;

Thence turns the brink an obtuse angle (seen
Where first appears the plunging face so green)
This angle follows then, far over runs,
Where deep the tumbling waters roll in tuns;
Another angle sharply turns down thence,
On, down the stream, still down and wide from hence,
Much more down stream than opposite to us;
Makes at the tower one angle more, obtuse,
(The round, stone tower, not built upon the sands,
That near Goat Island, near the brink there stands).
These are the brink's great lines; vast, numberless,
The details of its turns and crevices.

We stand close by the rush, amid the roar,
See near their brink the mighty masses pour.
There, far up stream, there from the clouds they troop,
Here, down, down, down, to unknown depths they swoop!
Look to the right, the left, across, down stream,
Still the gulf's walls, vast, widening, waters teem,
Half round th' horizon—falls seem not to end,
While to the zenith clouds of spray ascend.
A mile around this Horseshoe Fall may wind,
Ere by Goat Island in its course confined
Athwart the gulf—there on the other side—
'Twixt distant shores a faint line may divide—
Faint, far away, far water, farther sky;
To find the left shore there our eyes will try—
Three miles above it must be—is it lost,
Melted to clouds or mid the breakers tost?
There! singly see the quiet tree-tops peep,
A nearly level, tree-notched line thence sweep,
Till at our right it nears, curves up a bank, high, steep,
Whose level marks the level of the plain,
Rolling from which, Niagara's glories reign;
Then from the same far distant point, reversed,
The tumult growing as 't is more dispersed,

Another line sweeps on, turns to our feet,
A long, grand curve, notched by the waters' beat—
'T will fifty feet of gradual fall define;
Now if we mark the rocky brink's dark line,
Between these points, how high and wide the space,
How vast the field o'er which these rapids race!
Ledge after ledge the waters ride and leap,
Let loose, they now seem not one law to keep,
'Gainst sunken rocks they dash—then from them fly
Rosettes, sparkling like diamonds, twice, thrice ten feet
high—
This slope, remember, you by miles must measure,
Where they display with potent power their pleasure,
Where these wild rapids with each other cope,
In freaks beyond imagination's scope.
See! near our right turn with a sudden mind
That grand curve's waves, sharp, surging swift and blind,
Your flesh creeps as on rock and air they grind—
Hear! how they lap bloodthirstily the beach—
God help the living thing within their reach!
More palpable than all the power, extent,
Is there the fierce, the tigerish intent!
There, near the center frantically wild—
Our feet here laving gently as a child—
There roll they mammoth-like, huge, seeming slow—
Here o'er the riddled rock play to and fro,
Like little kittens ere too old they grow.

Study this foreground: we stand on a ledge,
A level rock, with lamellated edge,
Irregular and broken in its course;
The tiny wavelets with expiring force,
First lave our feet, then rippling, curling o'er,
Another level seek some two feet low'r;
They join a foaming stream, not wide nor deep—
We on yon lost and lonely rock could leap,

Oblong, rectangular, flat and quite dry,
When *up* Lake Erie whistling winds blow high;
But blowing down, the waters somewhat rise—
The prettiest play beneath God's glorious skies,
On, round this rock will then regale our eyes.
A heart seems to be beating far above,
Laving this lost rock with the pulse of love;
Gentle pulsations spread fold after fold,
In fashion infinite, in forms untold,
Bedeck it with such living tenderness,
Bestow such beauty with their soft caress,
So fringe, flow'r, furbelow, festoon this rock,
With such new antics still your knowledge mock,
And yet so meek, mild, modest in their way,
While on each side there is such wild display—
I think you will agree with me and say,
'T is very, very beautiful to see,
More beautiful it surely could not be!
The rushing stream 'tween this lost rock and us,
Its foam folds into folds most curious,
While leaping up beyond, another flies,
New flower-and-leaf-forms ever to devise.
Two ledges next above, each two feet higher,
Or less, with care observe and *then* admire;
Raise your eyes slowly—turn, extend your view—
Each inch of space startles with something new,
So utterly unthought of, quaint and queer—
And still surprised you still cry what is here?
There, waves fall plumb, there, farthest to the right,
Throb, throb and dart like jets of liquid light,
(Flash at right angles as they strike below,
Almost as swift as lightning thence they go)
Then (to the left) their movement change and glide
(Not dashed to foam) swift, swift and swifter slide—
Ridge o'er one ledge whose front they hardly hide;

This ledge, the upper, to the left extends,
More to the left and down from it descends
Slightly, a space, o'er which, not foaming still,
A new curve every line of room doth fill:
There—do you see waves turn, twist on their track,
When almost o'er that second ledge, fly back?
Curves infinite this strangest surface net,
While near the low'r ledge cones dance, dart and jet,
Forms indescribable still beauty fret—- —
Talk of invention! of idealizing!
You fool! first find the skill of realizing!
You profound mathematician, need you go,
Far as the stars that you may something know?
Here you can ponderingly calculate,
With complex conics fill your tapeline pate.
The rock whereon we stand and that lost one,
Where waves still dally ever and anon,
The lowest ledge beyond it, have one level;
The next below presents a foaming revel,
The waves there dash to squirming froth-heaps high—
Sometimes rosettes ten feet in th' air will fly—
But fronting that lost rock they are more quiet,
(It fronts the brink) there run not so much riot,
There refluent ripples seem disposed to rest,
To be inclined to snug into a nest;
Indeed, those flowing on soon form a place,
Smooth, like a polished, convex mirror's face,
Damasked by froth with delicacy's grace;
The spot is small; the impulse comes again,
From boisterous work they can not long refrain—
All, each and all, one purpose only prove—
Onward, resistless to the brink they move—
They overarch that brink in beauteous play,
In movement changed and floriform array,
Down slippery grooves here smooth and swift they glide,
With foaming light-crests there the edge bestride;

In yon spot they scoop out the flinty brink
So savagely they almost seem to think,
There o'er it dart in lines ferocious, straight,
And horrent fly into the face of fate—
At convex arching o'er the brink there hoot—
Direct into the yawning gulf there shoot—
Whew! how they cleave its ever-gaping maw!
These waves terrific are that curve's we saw—
Described above—here is their fury's height—
Here they seem biting out the rock outright!
So all and all, hurl, hurry, whirl and heave,
Till loosed still more, the brink they leap and leave,
Then suddenly far swifter, brighter grown,
With freedom such as they have never known,
Down, headlong hurtling down, and down, and down—
They glorious action now with glory crown!

Art pregnant busy brain with thoughts of power?
If life thou carry, be it born this hour.
Bear me no puling babe, no doughy brat—
I want no work indefinite like that.
Ah, words, ah, language, now, now do not fail;
Make not expression puny, poor and pale,
While I burn with an incandescent glow—
Tell something now of what I feel and know.
Here is a wondrous down and upward play—
Floods falling fast, and storms of mounting spray.
If greatly greatness 't is not mine to utter,
Ah, let me inane sacrilege not sputter!
Yet be my speech with delicacy clothed,
E'en as these Falls to beauty are betrothed.
Precipitated, undulations vast,
Move, as the Present moves upon the Past,
An irresistible, unbroken force,
While changeful hours conceal its awful course—

So o'er these hasting waters' ponderous powers,
An intermittent motion wreathes its flowers— —
Above, a great heart *must* beat, beat and beat—
A heart that moves a world's floods in its heat,
And whirls them on and on, so far, so deep,
They seem into another world to leap!
Throbbing and throbbing with a quickening jet,
Their path between two worlds they fringe and fret
With forms so exquisite, so tender, new,
Another new world hangs between the two!
Along the brink, rocks more or less depressed,
Less covered, more projecting than the rest,
Cause marked divisions o'er the waters' face,
Extending from the brink down to the base,
Their stubborn influence throughout you trace;
So the Past shapes the Present, Future still,
Let us be free as e'er we can or will.

Freedom, ah, freedom! all things love thee, all!
All leap to new life at thy witching call!
Let not a crowd's curse curse our country ever;
'T would be as fatal as its parts to sever;
Men, women, water, trees, all things want room,
To burst into their perfect, beauteous bloom;
With larger freedom all things lovelier grow—
When treasonous slavery struck its first foul blow,
The millions of the North flashed out in ire,
The black Rebellion to consume with fire.
Yet did it free them from that unwise bond
That bound their necks to slavery's magic wand;
Slowly but daily now their thoughts make fate—
This curse from out the land exterminate—
Spare nothing, white nor black, no shape, no thing,
That can such wicked, causeless treason bring;
All perish utterly, all DIE, DIE, *DIE*
Is the resolve our freemen now live by!

Hear! hear their voice! hear! hear their tread resound!
Lick up this slavery's rock which kept us bound—
Rest not till into nothingness 't is ground!
Nor rich, nor poor, proud, independent, free,
They give the law to their own liberty;
With hard, not slavish work good sense expand,
Each man of them a king on his own land.
The masses never reached a nobler pitch;
These rebels would now rot in their last ditch,
Had there but been a MAN to lead—alack!
God gives us leaders like that LITTLE MAC! (78)
Damnation dog that traitorous imbecile!
Oh, what contempt abhorrent do I feel
For puffed pretension in a puny man—
Brains bolted of all substance but the bran!
Seeing such men, who, who would be man from choice—
And yet to be a man who 'll not rejoice,
In glowing praises raise his grateful voice,
When men, the million, the suspected mass,
The freemen of the North all hopes surpass,
Are still enthusiastic, stern, intense,
Though they were doomed so long to dig defense,
When they could ride down all this Satan's brood,
And serve it up for turkey-buzzards' food— —
Like their Niagara, men, means still pour,
From out the mighty Northern reservoir,
Like their Niagara most truly great,
Most glorious while in that transition-state,
That bounding leaping toward the broader field
Their ocean-future only full can yield.

Thus leaps Niagara toward its broad ocean,
Thus burst its waves with beauteous, bright commotion,
Plunge from the rock that base no more will lend,
Expand in splendor as the air they rend;

If at the brink their depth in feet be two,
An hundred feet below 't is twenty through;
Far from the brink they arching shoot, observe,
And from this convex line they do not swerve,
Are farthest out when at their shifting base;
The line is not continuous; you can trace
The throbbing motion of that mighty heart,
E'en in the densest, thickest, greenest part,
While into jagged portions, torn, uneven,
In places of less depth this line is riven.
Yet is there nothing ragged, incomplete;
The shallowest places hang like a vast sheet
Of finest lace with heavy, pendent fringes,
Where the pulsation on the air impinges;
These fringes curve transversely, are convex below,
Downward more wide apart, defined and heavier grow;
In the turmoil we rather guess than see
That in the whole height thirty there may be,
For as they move, who counts as rapidly?
Thus seem they everywhere and yet nowhere,
Embroideries of flow'r forms, quaint and rare,
Snowdrops unnumbered for a moment peer—
Now vanish—are now there, now here—
Burst through that unique, gorgeous emerald green,
Surpassing for a moment e'en its sheen.
Far up the rapids mark dashed into light,
A stream of foam that poets would call white—
Flung o'er the brink in flowerets down the green,
Can many things more beautiful be seen?
Another, near the brink, there, farther on,
From sunken rocks the water 's dashed upon,
Springs bright and down the green profusely showers,
A double wreath of changing, brilliant flowers;
Converging where the center 's worn acute,
Far over, there 's these waters' gala suit;

The rocky brink there only they conceal,
Barely their garment's glorious green reveal—
Those center-waves, wild-frantic in their joy,
To deck ornately all their force deploy;
Lawns figured, flowered, of fine, rare woof display,
Fringe and festoon and garland and array
With lightsome movement, with light, living grace,
With brilliancy the waters' brilliant face!
  Ah no!
          Let me not say their gala-suit is there:
Seem they not still more beautiful elsewhere?
Between the center and the distant tower
Does not that, *that* look like their brightest flower,
The burst of beauty on their bursting splendor,
And oh, so sweetly, infinitely tender!
Ay, thus each moment, through each day and night,
By sun, by moon, by stars, or when their light
Is by the coursing cloud-hosts caught and sent to us,
Niagara grows ever still more beauteous!
One part exhausts my words—what can I do,
When one that seems still greater comes to view,
What else but say, when all my words are spent,
Not then and there, but here and now I meant,
When I said this, *this* is the glorious spot—
Ay, overwhelmed I cry, where is it not?
Behold, below the brink a rock projecting,
The waves from their appointed course deflecting,
Between the center and the tower, there throne,
On this, the western face, unique, alone,
Two, if not flying, yet foaming buttresses,
Two brilliantly dissolving brightnesses!
How busy too! hand over hand they climb,
Working fast, faster, faster against time,
They crook, squirm, leap, dart, jump, twist—how they try
Heels over head, back to the top to fly— —

Are they not beautiful in the endeavor
To do what still they can not do forever?
Thus endless beauty and exhaustless power
Go hand in hand until we reach the tower,
There more profusely novelty to shower.
  In the whole breadth of *this* Fall, only here,
Rocks on the brink and at the base appear;
To th' tower a foot-bridge from Goat Island leads
And no abutment artificial needs;
Just on the brink some rocky masses lie,
Between, not over which, the waters fly,
While from below, half up the fearful height,
Huge rocks are heaped up, where the jets alight,
Dart off in spray, or in cascades between
In endless, tortuous dashings can be seen.

  Change may not always be improvement, no;
These last rocks crashed into the gulf below,
I think it is now eighteen years ago,
And added beauty in a high degree;
But when the cliff adjacent—let me see—
Yes, two years since, tuns, tuns in weight down thundered,
Where the preceding year I drew, it blundered;
It gained in grandeur, for its beetling brow,
Is still more threatening, overlooming now;
IT, like a hero unacknowledged thrones
Who will not speak except in startling tones,
Nor till the ceaseless worry of this world
Has mined his patience and his being is hurled,
Haply against his will and yet in wrath,
Unto another place to cleave a path,
To make those hear who would not see before,
To break, but to be rugged still the more,
Yet show mayhap pure crystals to the core.
These rocks too buried my beloved cascade,
So wondrous, beautiful, and one that made

A fitting foreground for a scene so weird—
I meant to paint it, ignorance to beard.
I heard the crash and saw the cloud of dust
From where we stand—ay, Madam, do not trust
The rocks we 're on, I should before have said—
For quivering with these waters' mighty tread,
Almost beneath our feet soon after fell
Fragments disjointed, huge, and made a hell
Of sound if not of waters—out pell-mell
They rushed—the people—from their houses near,
Startled as if this were uncommon here.
And have a care too of a sudden mood,
The spray may take, its presence to intrude;
Subtle and penetrating is its reach,
Your dry-goods finery right well 't will bleach.
It always takes the color from yon green,
When but its least vagaries intervene,
When but a breath comes from some giant's throat,
Between that emerald and our eyes to float.
I told you of the falling waters' fringes,
Where the pulsation on the air impinges—
In many points their convex edges end—
From each of these fine particles ascend—
Expanded by the currents of the air—
Their shapes to comets some resemblance bear.
One source this of the spray; the other leaps,
Darts rocket-like, rolls up from unknown deeps—
If shallow, falling waves fling vails like lace,
So finely wrought that they no fairy's face
Of finest finished features could conceal—
Yet gauze-like weavings still more rare reveal
The movements infinite, the lighter play,
The weird, the magic mysteries of the spray!
Bedeviled dauber! not so much ado—
The Lord is criticized as well as you;

"The Falls is nice, but the spray spiles 'em," cries
Curtly a critic who consults his eyes;
"Spile 'em" no more, ye sprites! no longer spread
The sun-the moon-loved Iris-sisters' bed,
Ungrateful as these are—they flit as soon,
As instantly as they miss sun or moon;
Naught heed they of your playful tenderness;
Responsive are they to but one caress—
Their life, their burning glow, their trembling bliss,
Are only for their heavenly lovers' kiss!

When generous SHEARS was of the Clifton House the head, (79)
A traveling Englishman there petulantly said,
"Here in this country everything 's so *vaast*"—
True is the judgment he upon it passed;
And far more beautiful it must be too,
Than is the Old World if they tell us true.
Ruskin, who sees so well, sees o'er the Rhine,
A shuddering Iris on her damp sheets pine;
And beauteous Italy has cataracts
That furnish BYRON with most harrowing facts.
Behold poor Iris there! like hopeless hope,
O'er death-bed agonies most frightful mope;
All hell he finds and all its parts infernal,
Damnation is it—something that 's eternal—
Horror's essential oil will not suffice
To picture what he saw with his own eyes.
That cataracts must in his eyes have been
While writing thus is in the writing seen;
How damned delectable there falls must be,
Giving to poets such sweet imagery!
Dissection is an item I insist
Belonging to the death-bed, all-hell list,
The only truthful figure he has missed.

Vast falling waters not much honor pay
To human modesty found in their way;
Such modesty they, like the Lord will scorn,
Strip all who come as he still has them born.
Your drapery to Dame Nature's they will trim,
Your body they 'll enjoy with joy most grim,
They will dissect you, Madam, limb from limb
If you without or with your will intrude
On their most playful, their joy-maddened mood.
Could not a tiger tear you in his glee?
Let us be safe, he 's beautiful to see!
How lithesomely he leaps! how high he bounds!
If there are claws and teeth and warning sounds,
Yet long we not to join him in his gambols,
Though certain he would have us for his shambles?
Niagara 's like fascination dread—
To join the play around, below, o'erhead—
To be as noisy, wicked and as mad,
To be as busy, boisterous and as glad!
  On God serene as soon seek for a scowl,
On heaven's great glory look for hell-flames foul,
As raw-heads, bloody-bones, things of that kind,
On our Niagara expect to find;
Niagara! how beautiful thy face!
There nothing of the "horrible" has place!
  Come to this spot, my friend, some day in June,
July or August, two, three hours past noon,
The zenith, west, southwest quite clear must be—
Then wealth of color may be here to see.
May be: for these conditions sometimes fail
These colors' most extraordinary scale,
All their unrivaled vividness to show—
I have not found yet why this should be so.
  That Lake Superior, all the upper lakes indeed,
Are well nigh colorless all seem agreed,

Except the last above The Falls, Lake Erie,
Where forces are at work and never weary—
Lime, vegetable matter decompose,
(For this I cite John Locke as one who knows)
Thicken the water that you can not peer
More than four feet below the surface here.
Impure in fact yet in appearance pure,
It seems done purposely to make it sure,
The color of these Falls should matchless be,
As is their action, form, immensity.
  Perhaps your untaught eyes may not discern
The tints when there: some this takes years to learn—
Yet if a cloud throw shadow on yon green,
When it by you is for the first time seen,
Then passing on, its place give to the sun,
You may exclaim as others then have done,
Had we not seen, this we had not believed!
(How frequently are daubers thus aggrieved)
E'en you, unskilled, a change may then discover—
Of Nature's looks need be no zealous lover
To see that green put on its gold-green robe—
Haply none other like it on the globe—
  The peerless sun, the palpitating dome,
Find here the welcome of a happy home;
How they with eager rivalry contend,
Harmoniously opposing natures blend,
This field magnificent of rapids share!
When the sun's fiery eyes are burning there,
The dome's blue orbs still peer out everywhere;
When yellow, orange, burnished gold appear
The cool blue hues from clear sky still are near;
When rocks with ruby, topaz tints are flaming,
Their ardor shades of amethyst are taming;
The dim rock-brink, the sun, the water, sky,
Melt yonder to a royal purple dye;

Pale-pink, cream-green, prismatic touches tinge
The froth-and-foam-flowers as they ledges fringe;
Veins like bright molten gold are darting through
Waves of dark golden-green and purple blue;
That strangest surface with such varied lines,
In each of them a different tint defines.
Rocks here, when dry, are pale-pink, pearly-gray—
Touched by a wavelet or a sprite of spray,
To precious stones of every hue they turn—
Then flashing diamonds in profusion burn—
Then rubies' blood-red, topaz' richest yellow
The greenish beryl and blue sapphire mellow.
Our loved, lone, lost rock lies a stone inlaid,
Those streams a mother-of-pearl bed have made,
This beauteous bed with brilliant gems is teeming,
Thick from its wreaths their tinted eyes are gleaming;
Fronting this rock—that quiet place you know—
A like show-case can lapidary show?
And this loved rock, love's wavelets loving laving,
When sun and sky their painting wands are waving,
They seem to center more affection there—
Touch *it* with an inimitable care.
Now fast as love takes it in its embrace,
See, sun and sky, how they each other chase
And with a rapid skill unrivaled trace
The yellows, oranges, reds, purples, blues,
The violets in all their various hues—
What silver-pearl-like chaplets fast are flung,
Round curving, crowding wavelets richly strung,
And how the sun its fire-breath nowise stints,
The sky its kiss with cooling lips imprints— —
Turn from the right now to the left (half round
You know you turn to see its farthest bound
Across the gulf where we Goat Island found)
The tower this jutting point shall tower-fall name;
Deservedly it would have world-wide fame,

If not a world of waters with it fell
That would keep Byron busy bawling hell:
How small this section with the whole compared!
Yet boundless beauty it has amply shared:
Pale-pink 's the common flag of foam and spray,
Reviewed in person by the god of day;
But there the teeming and tumultuous crowds,
Though all else yield to domineering clouds,
In darkest days still to their colors cling,
Pale-pink though paler to pale pearl-green bring;
But when, oh heavens! how marvelous is the change,
From sunlight clouded to its unchecked range—
Lit by the sun's life-light-love lending glance,
How proudly all in precious colors prance,
How with the sun all into new life start—
New swarms of spray-sprites leap and dance and dart
Dressed in gay robes arranged with finest art—
That rich foam-light a glamour-garb assumes,
In dreamy cream-green, pearl-pink strangely blooms;
These are the rocks—you may remember them—
That fell and of this tower-fall made this gem—
Set in that rarest, deep-green river-bed,
How they contrast their golden-ingot-red— —
An eddy up stream drives the current here,
And leaves the water from light froth-foam clear,
Its waves around these rocks play hide and seek,
While they lie ever motionless and meek;
If mid this joy-commotion there be grief,
Tears coursing o'er these rocks bring its relief;
They weep that they can not return caresses,
That wave and spray-love ever effervesces;
And yet sometimes do they not seem to spring,
To leap to sunshine, join the bounding ring,
The whirl of action, form, sound, color, light,
Where not a single death's-head comes in sight,

No rocks Byronic look black all around,
With "pitiless horror" our souls confound—
No! no! no! glories only here abound!
On our Niagara there 's nothing sooty,
'T is clothed in Color's iridescent beauty!
Color, impalpable, pervading, weird—
What would this world be if by thee not cheered—
And our Niagara thy subtle skill,
Decks with unbounded love, unbridled will!

Let us now leave and love this charmed tower-fall;
Of the whole western face a part how small—
The distance to yon central point how great!
How breadth, height, color, splendor, motion mate!
From the far sky, dim, faint in clearest view,
The rapids course in greenish-purplish blue,
While pearl-pink foam-light terraces defines,
In varied, delicate and level lines;
Deeper and deeper as the brink they near,
These colors grow, though ever bright and clear,
Then merge into the rock-brink's red and gold—
This passed, what brilliant beauty is unrolled!
When foam-light flings its fairy laces o'er,
Their dazzling brightness color does not low'r—
Its touch ethereal, color seems no longer—
The slightest breath of pink may prove the stronger—
Descending low'r, lace-meshes wider grow,
There the least purplish-gray would seem to show;
But when above the brink the tumult 's less,
Below the brink, how great the tenderness
Color in emerald green can there express.
Alternately in large and well-marked masses,
Whose splendor haply all on earth surpasses,
This breath of pink, this tender green divide,
Yet keep the breadth throughout this breadth so wide,

So vast, diminishing to us its height;
Its low'r third too is of dense spray the site,
Whose rolling volumes higher can seldom rise,
And lessening thus its great height to our eyes;
This varies much; its breadth unequaled never;
The waters in their new bed do not sever
From beauty, nay they emulate their past:
And e'en their movement is almost as fast;
First mid the nether spray high hillocks heave,
Then can not stay an instant—they must leave—
From shore to shore, except that rock-bed green,
Froth-foam-light, of a cooler, silvery sheen,
Flies to complete the breadth of this grand scene—
The yellow sunlight floods its perfect face,
Spirits of roses red then leave their trace,
From the blue dome descends attempering grace—
Spray-sprites aloft majestically soar,
Painting bright phantasies on heaven's blue floor;
Some seem such souls as need not be forgiven
Who see already their new home in heaven;
The glory of this scene to heaven they bear,
Glory that may not shame the glories there;
See how they change yon isle to fairy-land—
Yonder behold that crowding, busy band,
Bearing the sun-loved Iris as she trembles,
Her joy of life and love to none dissembles—
A wondrous witch! how deep her colors' glow—
In tone to brilliant foam-light far below,
Yet the most brilliant object is her bow;
But often variable: here is she coy,
A glow of glory there, a glorious joy,
Where light and color all their power combine,
With splendor e'en the splendors here outshine,
A glimpse of heaven's illumination give,
Tempting a cynic to rejoice to live— —

Let now large castellated cumuli,
(Thrice ten degrees, not more, they must be high)
Crowd teeming tribute from God's glorious sky
Between Goat Island and Canadian shore,
Above the rapids looming, leaning o'er,
Loom and lean o'er these waters as if they
Longed their own place to leave in this display,
To fall into this fascinating strife,
To be as active, eager, full of life—
Who, though in all their bearing so subdued,
Seldom seen vivid here, though richly hued—
Still are they glorious e'en where splendors shine,
Splendors more dazzling, if not more divine—
Splendors so full, fresh fullness ever teeming,
I sometimes doubt, dream, deem it but a dreaming—
Ha! seems it not like a sublime endeavor,
Whose soul would seize and whirl yours on forever!
Ha! flush you not with fervor at this strife,
Fullness of form, sound, color, splendor, life?
Do you not feel you could do anything?
Into this vortex bound with one mad spring,
To ride on joy-delirium's whirling wing?
What if your lovely limbs be laved to death—
Your spirit would be loosed to boundless breath!
You would float finely, Madam, at yon height—
In size you think your little hand now right,
To do the work of any proud spray-sprite?
Ethereal color's still more nimble corps,
You could help them paint all this fretwork o'er,
With pencil exquisite bring into view
The work invisible these spray-sprites do?
Ha! mingling in their moonlight mysteries,
How you could learn most secret histories—
Learn how enchantments on enchantments rise,
To be admired by more than mortal eyes—

Learn to interpret music-words that course
Through my poor frame with an unearthly force—
And though I listened as a lover would,
And thought some whisperings I understood,
And feathery touches thrilled me—by my beard!
Sad maiden-sprites my wooing wildly jeered!
Yet listening to these sounds that do not stun,
Do you not hear through the confusion One,
One burden and One song—all with One Voice,
Or low or loud, in unison, REJOICE!
Each movement surging and each ripple curling,
Thousands of giants tramping, stamping, whirling,
The ponderous pounding and the pretty purling,
What power, what praise, what joy must they not tell!
If you will listen lovingly and well,
Haply you 'll hear mid its triumphant roar,
The low, low lullaby of love's loved lore—
Then thundrous, crack! crack! crack! comes crashing o'er
Your ears a sound that gives each nerve a jar,
And makes you wonder where and what you are;
How much through one unpracticed sense we lose!
The whirls of sound that our dense ears confuse,
Had but BEETHOVEN'S spirit heard them sing—
How o'er the world forever they would ring!
Earth's fullest chorus to God's Gloria—
To Him its heavenly high Hallelujah—
The anthem of its ONE NIAGARA!

The scene Church painted I have now depicted;
It is to this my couplets are restricted;
With few more words I leave this work of God,
The work of man, if possible, to laud.
Madam, if I had money and a bride,
I'd sometime at the Clifton House abide,
And take my rooms along its eastern side,

Where th' American Fall could charm my eye—
Then I would have my love so sit and lie,
That its fine lace should be her bright background,
Its beauty should her beauty all surround,
Fit bridal vail for my rapt soul's sweet care
Blushing responses to my glances there—
I tremble nigh with terror at such bliss— —
Now, Madam, fail not to remember this:
Those who Niagara's extent would know,
Must tread its leading points above, below;
Hire a carriage and then be sure to walk—
I wish I could be with you still and talk—
Talk of Goat Island and the rare, rare taste
That will not make of it an "improved" waste;
Long live the PORTER family, by whom (81)
'T is kept in all its pristine, perfect bloom,
A gem set on these waters' tossing breast,
So still, so quiet and so full of rest,
I hardly know sometimes which I love best;
And all the little isles, romantic nooks,
Laved by most gentle, murmuring little brooks;
And I would like to see this heaving tide
In the abyss, to a smooth calm subside,
Then dash on suddenly, as if t' outdart
The earth itself, had it but had the start—
How wonders great still one another follow,
How at the whirlpool it itself doth swallow,
(So guide-books say) and how at last there lies,
Blended and blessed with our God's glorious skies,
Blue-green, faint, distant, an immense expanse
That leads the soul afar into a trance,
That magnet-like draws on the dreamy gaze—
ONTARIO, in midsummer's morning haze— —

PART IV.

CHURCH'S NIAGARA now bring before us:
"Have you seen Church's picture?" was the chorus
When at Niagara I daubed in fifty-eight—
I saw it since in Gotham, and can say 't is great!
Great in invention! in the grand Ideal!
It scorns the "nauseous detail" of the Real!
How nicely Nature's motion here is trimmed,
How all her glaring show is gently dimmed;
The water, if it move at all, moves on
With all the easy nonchalance of ton,
Observes the rules of good society,
Falls with Fifth Avenue propriety.
One form, repeated in a happy way,
Simplicity of genius doth display;
For that most varied, strange foreground's array,
This picture gives the same touch—dab—dab—dab—
Is it a wonder that our critics blab?
Its color and its light (a thought how great!)
Into two bits of rainbow concentrate—-—
In short, all Church's work unrivaled stands,
By man, or dead or living in all lands,
To bring the grandest subjects to the smallest scale—
Therefore fit monarch for our Art-world him we hail!

Yet in Niagaras he 's almost shamed
In his own way, by two who 're not so famed—
By GEO. L. BROWN and R. S. DUNCANSON—— (82) (83)
Some very curious things the Lord has done:
He made Niagara--then made this trio,
Church, Brown and Duncanson! Rejoice Ohio!
Of these great painters of Niagara,
Thy colored son deserves the most *eclat.*
I think the Lord felt he must try his patience,
By not inflicting well-earned castigations
On fellows who should round the world be scourged,
That it of blasphemy like theirs be purged!

My leisure fails me here; more facts I could compress,
Were almost all our Art not worse than nothingness.
This prince of humbugs, this great gasbag Church,
Our *writers* have put up on his high perch.
In Art (excuse the phrase) they "go it blind;"
Take the ATLANTIC MONTHLY; there you 'll find:
"Church AND TURNER!" ye gods and little fishes! (84)
But don't they serve us up some curious dishes!
And wot you not what has become of him,
The meek man Moses, limber too of limb,
High on a hill and painted by friend Page?
You call that queer work great in phrases sage,
Write yourselves down chief asses of the age.
You puff *artist*-photographers to get
Scenes wanting in your *art*-collection yet;
Old woman's twaddle on the stereoscope,
Proves that you blindly through creation grope,
But for your blindness chatter all the louder,
Swearing there 's nothing fit to eat but chowder;
But I've no time to waste on words like yours;
It is a gabbling nothing ever cures;
ATLANTIC Monthly! H'm! you're not knee-deep,
Nor is there salt enough in you to keep.

Art in the NEW YORK TRIBUNE shines as bright,
With like long ear-appendages bedight;
My good friend Page I might have passed in quiet,
If dunder-pates in folly ran not riot.
"Italian peasants" I think it was called,
Where Page our eyes astounded and appalled;
Greeley's Art-editor this strange thing praised,
And proved the critic and the painter crazed—
A great, great picture he cried out amazed.
I'll not conceal that I owe him a grudge,
This self-appointed, blatant, high Art judge.
"The name of Frankenstein," he tried to sneer,
"Connected with Niagara we hear!" (85)
Then the vile thing in private matters grubbed,
For which the Gotham daubers got well snubbed;
What do you know, BRUTE-FOOL! what do you know
Back to your kennel with your fetid flow!
Back to your kennel! dare not bring again
Your carious carcass among decent men!

GREELEY! your back shall not escape my whip;
You are responsible for this—come, strip!
For pictures, poetry, for pious tracts,
You have no fancy; you want stubborn facts.
I'll give you some: I've worked as hard as you
Through all my life at what I had to do;
I've been as earnest, faithful, diligent,
On good work only all the while intent;
Nor wealth nor office have I sought and gained,
Of which at least the first you have obtained;
If in political mud-pools you find
The suitable contentment for your mind,
Though you see naught in Nature nor in Art,
Aside from your quite profitable part,
You should respect the earnestness you feel,
On other earnest men not put your heel;

If ignorant of Art, are you of men?
Why to spitvenom give your columns then?
You are too busy with the awful cares
Of nations, armies and like grand affairs,
"On, on to Richmond!" you must daily yelp,
Like any half-drowned, half-blind, unlicked whelp,
You can not stop your office well to rule,
While you tell LINCOLN he is but a fool!
Nay, see the force of habit! your large talk
Of earnestness, of extra upright walk,
So long imposed on us, sticks to my pen—
And this I have to take all back again.
'T is now believed by those who were your friends,
With public virtue you mask private ends;
Of a triumvirate the jackass, you
Were fed on thistles by the other two, (86)
Sometimes a noxious Weed you got to chew;
The public crib they closed to your sharp hunger:
Now as you thought yourself chief freedom-monger,
You kicked the traces in an ugly fit—
Come, tell us—how much have you made by it?
Weeds will choke all the seed that you can sow,
Meanwhile in you we now all learn to know
Not the sincere, impracticable dreamer,
But the incompetent, the foiled, sore schemer—

Come! be by searching truth's tribunal tried!
Come forth! if you've got sober since you died,
You, drunken mad-dog, EDGAR ALLAN POE— (87)
Is it my fault that I must call you so?
Your works, like you, are born of alcohol;
Horrid monstrosities, distortions all;
It needs no doctor's gallipot or jar,
Filled with that stuff, to keep them as they are;
Soaked with its strange and strong, insidious power,
Your tales the many eagerly devour;

The Barnum of the Western Museum, FRANKS, (88)
Here for apt illustration shall have thanks;
He fitted up a noted murderers' room,
Of victims, too, which they sent to the tomb,
Wax figures with authentic, gaping gashes,
The weapons that made all these hideous slashes;
An hundred dollars covered the expense—
Three thousand dollars was his recompense!
You, Poe, through all your nature most debased,
You pandered to this craving tiger-taste;
King Alcohol through you once ruled our realm
Of literature, you staggered at its helm;
By English critics, too, were recognized,
A fact which was by us most highly prized.
You, with an impudence sublimely brazen,
In Art your frantic fumes must largely blazon;
Here I've a crow to pick with you, my friend—
Your poor, poor raven that rhymes without an end?
No, mad dog, no! but do you recollect
How at my pictures once you picked and pecked?
They were done soberly, with anxious care,
No time, no labor on them did I spare,
All *that* nigh any fool could have seen there;
Nor was the labor lost, they were well painted;
Then *you*, with every fiber liquor-tainted—
You, YOU, who all your life could not walk straight,
With swaggering ignorance my work berate?
When in the gutter the last time you lay,
When death, disgusted, almost turned away,
When you with rot-gut whisky dying stunk,
And thus into God's presence reeled DEAD-DRUNK—
I tell you, mad dog, when I heard all this,
I helped outraged humanity, to hiss!
You need not say now nothing should be said,
That I am living and that you are dead—

You drink yourself to death; must I forego,
Be balked of justice and revenge? Not so;
In prose to prick me you chose your own time,
And I choose mine to pay you back in rhyme;
Avaunt! and *nevermore* to me come nigh—
I do believe you stink of whisky yet—good bye!

RALPH WALDO EMERSON! does not that roll!
There ought to be some grand things in his poll!
And what he writes has volumes of big sound,
It seems at least, if 't is not clear, profound;
He writes Art-essays; stumbles right and left,
Imparts no sense, yet is of sense bereft;
A funny way he has to dignify
Art-matters in the reading public's eye:
That Newton with a tube stuck through the roof,
Makes out that stars spin round, is ample proof,
Sir Isaac from all Art can stand aloof;
What is so fine in foolish Pembroke's eyes,
Illimitable greatness may despise;
Greatness serene, sublimely, calmly cool,
Surely *it* can afford to play the fool;
Of course; of course, too, Emerson's fine sense,
Extols the "stone-dolls" smart impertinence; (89)
And all the while, One called our God looks on,
Knows every grain of sand, each sparrow gone—
HE may give "stone-dolls" an approving nod—
If so, excuse HIM, HE is only God—
While great Sir Isaacs his creation overlook—
Ralph Waldo Emersons vast nothings talk and book—
These flesh-dolls deign to deal but in THE LARGE — —
The Lord poor little things must take in charge.

I could write on and never reach the end,
Poor Art from these wiseacres to defend;

That female fellow Fanny Wright was smart, (90)
When she declared that, knowing naught of Art,
Naught would she write ; and it was too, most gracious,
When in all else she proved so contumacious.
Art-knowledge, knowledge of dear Nature's looks,
Ruskin alone perhaps shows in his books.

Young man ! would you to Art devote your life ?
Would you be minus babies and a wife,
Resign cash, sympathy, position too,
Have every dunce turn up his nose at you
Who waxes rich with rise of real estate,
Who onions, beans, pork, whisky learns to rate,
Who in man's lowest wants can speculate,
Ay, getting rich, can found an upper class,
Though he sold whisky at three cents the glass,
Where wealth thus gotten he may haply mix
With rich steam-doctors and their number six ;
Where moneyed cobblers smattering of law, (91)
The dunghill's top claim as the soundest straw ;
Where prime and mess pork-maggots put on airs,
And take low life with them up stairs ;
Where pettifoggers, wrangling all their lives,
May get the daughters of such folk for wives,
(I ne'er saw one for whom I'd give a fig
Inside of her expensive, dowdy rig)
But this, the pure Elysium of *elite*,
This happy mixture savory and sweet,
This most refined and elegant *bon-ton*,
A dauber do you think dare look upon ?
I say to you, young man, lay down your brush,
Art maddens all the minds it can not crush,
Now, now alas ! for you it is still worse
Than e'er before, still greater is its curse ;
Let me conjure you, heed the words I say,
And leave at once cursed Art's accursed way.

Now by photography's conceited pride,
What 's wanted of cheap portraiture 's supplied,
The only crib at which true Art might feed,
The snouts and feet of beasts of basest breed,
Are crowding with characteristic greed.
Result legitimate! hear on, young man!
Learn more facts why all Art I'd have you ban!
Years since a daub, painted they said by West,
Our papers puffed as if they were possessed;
And so they were—of twenty cents a line,
Each time they let the showman say 't was fine,
And made his words their own: Dick L'Hommedieu (92)
Owned part of the Gazette (a right good fellow too)
We—he and I—spoke with a little heat—
I claimed they were compelled their words to eat—
Said he: "We had the best of it, I think,"
He struck his pockets and I heard them chink—
"We got the dimes! But come—let 's take a drink!"
Excited by this picture-war, I made
An effort at Christ-pictures that ne'er paid.
The first I painted caused quite a sensation—
An accident—not an appreciation.
Day after day the crowds rushed in to see;
To all I tendered affability.
I asked e'en Littleworth to come; he came,
He bolted in, no greeting brought, no shame,
Shuffled a bee-line for the picture quick,
And with his dirty paw felt if 't was slick.
Our papers praised my picture quite as much
As they had done the bogus West botch-touch,
And every body said my road was clear
To fame and fortune, and that they were near.
None bought, none ordered pictures though, not one;
For many months I still worked on and on,
Till sickened to the very heart, I swore
Never to paint Christ-pictures any more.

Nick Littleworth pushed his poor drunken pet,
Whose SOULEless daubs will to the garret get, (93)
As will the work of all he recommended;
I can afford to laugh; though thus befriended
Are his poor pets now better off than I—
Was it worth more to fawn than to defy?
So fashion flocks, led by some goose or gander,
Yet wretched Art! *it* pays not e'en to pander!
Among these people I had a few friends;
But every thing to fashion's dictum bends;
When they their portraits wanted, they too went
Where Littleworth, not Art, sweet graces lent—
Oh *Lord!* that *block*head! was 't for you 't was meant?
Some of my oldest friends their walls have filled,
At large expense, with judgment all unskilled—
Pictures of note they bought—none such had I;
What matter then if I was left to die.
And other friends I have in whose sage view
Now photographs I should be painting too. (94)
A little man with but a little head,
And nothing in it—so somebody said—
Has a big Art-shop of photography,
Therefore my master in all Art must be.
('Mong our photographers he is the only one
Who has enough to do—gets funny fashion's run)
This little chap would stand behind my chair
And snarl: "What 's that! that 's not *skin-color* there!"
Young man! how I have worked to play this part!
At last, thank God! could I not reach HIGH ART?
This puny fellow, with his puny brain,
And he has not enough to get insane,
Who in all other work he tried but failed,
Without an effort he High Art has scaled,
Without a look at Nature, or a thought
Beyond the money to his pockets brought;

This BABY-BOOBY, standing by my chair,
Would snap: "What 's that! that 's not *skin-color* there!"
For such 's his phrase to those who paint for him,
And able men must heed his every whim;
Unless a miracle soon interpose,
Such destiny my Art-career must close,
Digestion's happy process to keep up,
On photographic diet I must sup,
Gulp Baby-booby's soul-destroying dictation,
Or in the *next* world try to dodge damnation.
I am bedeviled till I am benumbed,
'T is strange that I have not long since succumbed.
How with enthusiasm must I not be fired,
When so much of my brother's time and work 's required,
A picture of Niagara, portraying
The laws that falling waters are obeying,
By slow subscription to dispose of—well,
I should be glad that *somehow* it will sell
At less than half 't is worth, the truth to tell:
For money or your life my landlord cries,
Rent due for thirty months his patience tries?
One hundred, yes, and fifty dollars due—
Enormous the amount! nay, he'll not sue,
But tells me plainly I must leave my den:
Now look at the consistency of men!
Who is to blame for this? through all this time,
His agent nor himself asked for a dime;
And he was kind a year since—so I wrote—
But this he chokes, his hand 's now at my throat;
Yes, he was kind a year since; now how changed!
A picture, it was at that time arranged,
Should pay my rent; hate of photography I waived,
That from the clutches of this debt I might be saved;
The photographs he promises to send—
He leaves, he writes not—but now brings the end.

"I have determined to make this room pay;"
Not one word of the picture does he say.
I ask him: "Oh, I thought I'd let that go."
(It would have paid the rent another year or so,
E'en at the doubled rate; on money may he thrive
The paying which may me to desperation drive)
I tried to change his purpose; no appeal
Could make his hardened heart, RENT-FRANTIC, feel;
I hate my daubs and models; there they stood,
Were impotent to do me any good;
Yet seemed to say we'd help you if we could!
This man 's one of that inconvenient kind,
Who make a bargain and then change their mind;
He 's one of those who use an obligation
Which they confer, to work your degradation,
And yet can talk of merit's elevation.
* * * * * is my landlord's name; (96)
He changed, nor are my lines of him the same;
When last he came, had you been by, young man,
Beneath good manners his rough soul to scan,
You would have felt it was the devil's doing,
To put it in your head Art to be wooing!
I've worked enough to pay my way twice over,
For this, for any dirty world's best clover;
Ay, to society I'm not in debt;
Some petty sums to persons I owe yet—
If I shall ever, ever be so blest
To pay these, principal and interest,
No other favor will I ask of God
Than that I never, never may be trod
Into the dirt again by my own kind,
Who leave th' infernal furies far behind.
Hear more: men give me little work to do—
That little they 're so slow to pay for, too;
The pittance sometimes seems delayed by fate—
God! I have learnt to labor and to wait!

Necessity 's the measure of my wants,
No squandering of means my conscience haunts;
If work contracted for that I have done
Throughout my life for which th' accounts still run,
Had but been paid for, I could have escaped
My soul by hobnailed soles being badly scraped,
By those for whom I can not find a name—
Dogs, *brutes*, thrice, ten times BRUTES is true but tame—
Their number also swells the human shame—
See! COMSTOCK! anaconda-like would rush
Unlooked-for on me, all my bones to crush,
To slaver me with slime, swallow me whole—
My boyhood friend appoints this for my *rôle!*
'T is horrible! those I'd love more, they too,
Have made me feel that there was nothing true.
Had I been paid for work I've done, I say,
I should swear less, be more inclined to pray,
And of pestiferous debt be rid this day.
Ring, ding ding dong ding ring ring ding dong ding
"Walk to the cap'n's office please and settle,"
Or else my Muse may scald you in her kettle.
  One fellow though deserves not any grace:
You know Nick Littleworth delayed my case
In court e'en after he had turned a shade—
I gained it, but the money 's not yet paid. (97)
Defendant went to war, and we shall see,
Since he himself has no integrity,
Therefore that of the country to preserve,
He must have leisure if he has not nerve.
To get my pay I sued JOHN H. PIATT,
For what I painted five years since—near that;
His own dear self it was; a touch or two
May now make it more lovely yet still true.
Plaintiff, defendant in Ohio can
Swear hard that each is much the better man.

This fellow's insolence I could forgive,
His baseness to defraud me could outlive,
But when he swears that all I swear 's a lie,
I swear by heaven! I will not pass it by.
My hard-earned dollar thus he'd swear from me—
Out to the public with his perjury!
Let infamy 'mong men his portion be—
Its red-hot tire I clap around his soul,
Through life from youth to age now let him roll!

Sore is my spirit with such petty ravage;
And yet you would not, would you, get so savage!
Off and away my soul in thy balloon!
This grubby globe thou canst not leave too soon;
Rise! rise beyond this round of dust and mud,
To where worlds made of light in millions bud!
Yet look a moment o'er earth's fading scene—
Hear how truth throttles words awed by the mean—
Hear how men *talk* God, Love, Eternal Life,
See how they act a greedy, bloody strife;
See, see how wearing, anxious ardor sweeps,
Each one who can some dirt to little heaps—
(The dirt I scrape together I must eat—
E'en then the dimes will not make both ends meet)
See how they hug their heaps with trembling arms,
Proving a lie their speech of heaven's great charms;
Then shouldst thou spy another grub I hate,
Please drop a bag of ballast on his pate;
Then sailing on, leave littleness behind,
Then all resolved into a dreamy mind,
Let me still on, still farther, farther float—
To regions still more, more and more remote—
Till thrilled with rapture never known before,
I feel at last that deadening doubt is o'er,
I feel at last that long-sought, longed-for lore—

I feel the fanning of that mighty motion,
Its ether lap me like a living lotion— —
Down, down with him to earth, presumptuous worm!
Here is his place to curse, to creep, to squirm.
What, what has *he* to do with things above—
Send down the slave! give him a headlong shove!
He o'er the rest of us would lift his head—
We 'll show him something different instead—
He like the lark to soar till lost to sight—
He swim in splendor's surging sea of light—
He sing Love, Glory, Goodness and a God—
If *he* mounts he shall carry up the hod!
Be not in such a hurry; I'll come back;
I'll bear and if I can, inflict the rack;
My brow must still be plowed by bloody brogans,
And my poor soul still furrowed by Grub-Grogans,
By contumely I must be still ignored,
Still maddened must my ire on men be poured;
Yet why, alas! to none I would think harm—
How inexpressible is not the charm
When sweet good-nature from the human face
Beams kindly on me with its heavenly grace!
The little children! how I love them yet!
I can not live without a little pet—
Since I'll not grieve, for that is want of sense,
My brain sinks into cold indifference,
Or burns with a satiric, vengeful lust,
Not that it wills it, but because it must.
I try to do good work; I try to please;
The more I try the more they snarl and teaze;
I've walked the streets distracted all the night,
I tried to think if I was doing right— —
And do you ask me why I stay so long
Where true Art is not valued at a song,
Where I at last am kicked into the street,
And from a den to which few would retreat,

Where I, a strict, enthusiastic student,
Have not one habit to be called imprudent?
Nay, go into our Sanitary Fair, (98)
And take a look at some grand portraits there.
Am I so rusty in anatomy,
Or do some people change prodigiously—
Those portraits Longfellow's, Murdoch's? those men, (99)
When I last saw them, had their clothes on then,
And yet their human shape through tailor's skill
Discernible, yea quite distinct was still;
But T. BUCHANAN READ'S and HEALY'S Art—
And that with us is a distinguished part—
From the poor tailors snatches the great prize,
The human form completely to disguise—
Disguise! no, no, not that! but to disfigure!
Wrathful disgust! hide not thy righteous rigor!
'Mong all our shameless daubs there are none bigger!
'T is inconceivable what men may do
Till the enormity 's confronting you!
Is that Longfellow's face? I ought to know it—
On canvas once I took some pains to show it;
Murdoch! read Read just as he is of late,
For he deserves from you no better fate.
Young man! you, candidate for Art, hear on!
From other facts more lessons you may con.
These men, Read, Healy, of good minds, mature,
Do work that proves *nothing* our Art can cure.
Both breathed our buoyant, free, expanding air,
In Europe too, drew inspiration there—
Yet see, what are they? something 's wrong somewhere!
They paint no photographs; but I would rather drudge
For Baby-booby, let him of "*skin-color*" judge,
Than smear like Healy gross anomalies,
Or Read-like bend to worse inanities!
THOMAS J. GALLAGHER! my good old friend, (100)
Have you lost all your bones—oh heaven forefend!

Slick, soft, you simper, oh you 're very nice--
No other way you'd look at any price—
Read leaves out "vulgar detail" and the man,
And paints you, pleases you as none else can?

Haply in Sculpture we shall find no names
Whose fame our Art and common sense defames?
Ralph Waldo Emerson declares our race may yet,
Like Newton, far beyond this childish sculpture get;
Doctors differ: NATHANIEL HAWTHORNE tells us
That being almost born in clothes compels us
Only to deal in portrait-busts, and therefore
The Art of Sculpture is already done for. (101)
I do not know; but it does seem too bad,
When of no harm I think, but feel so glad
The prints from Palmer's Captive to behold, (102)
With child-like glee its beauties see unfold,
And take sweet comfort that she has no clothes
To sweep up—ay, what every body knows—
Defiling thus those feet and ankles, legs,
With filth that comes quite near its very dregs— —
I say it seems too bad to have a mind,
That these nice people may not think refined,
Like our Academy ladies—that fat one—
They 're vastly exercised the nude to shun,
And prove by clamor where their thoughts still run;
The mother can not feed her little pet,
Whose tiny tongue has learnt no talking yet,
Without offending, shocking baby's sight,
And if she wash it, hers must get a fright;
Had but the Lord shaped us like baby's doll—
Nay, we should then miss all this fol-de-rol!

PALMER! I will ask no man to pursue
What I think he or soon or late must rue;
But *if* they in a decent way will let you live,
Such work as yours I'll hail as long as you will give.

Flaming in capitals conspicuous,
One RANDOLPH ROGERS we must now discuss.
To Randolph Rogers, (that too sounds quite big,)
Nathaniel Hawthorne gives the great man's rig.
'T is in the preface to the Marble Faun, (103)
He not being born in them, such clothes gets on,
An ill-made suit that can not hide the clown;
He strutted in it here in our big town—
Thus preface-labeled By Authority,
Some of our daubers feasted him, hee! hee!
I'm glad and do not think it is a sin,
That Popkins was by him well taken in;
The scale of patron and of patronized,
Is very happily here equalized.
The Capitol's extension has large doors,
Whose bass-reliefs are some of this chap's chores;
I have not seen them and I need not see,
With Uncle Sam's collection they agree
No doubt in happy imbecility.
I'm past the angry point; I can not hoot:
Come Cuffy, you know where, apply your boot—
This rascal 's worse than Church! quick, kick him out!
How dare you, Hawthorne, send this scrub about!
Do let me ask you where this is to stop?
Prime beef you advertise and give us slop?
Your eyes are so untaught, you can not tell
The miserable from the master's spell?
I saw some of your pet pig's rooting here—
They called that making portrait-busts, oh dear!
Or haply, Hawthorne, you might never nose
The cunning that could on your mind impose—
The work on those bronze doors may have been wrought
By able, poor men whom his money bought:
If they are well done this must be the case—
I'll not believe yet man could be so base,

Could prostitute all art, all manhood so—
From truly good work fall so far below—
Could decency so utterly contemn—
Had he of true Art's garment touched the hem,
As Randolph Rogers with his modeling tool!
I state the simple facts, am calm and cool,
Only he must not take me for a fool.
The sculptor-hero of your Marble Faun,
Friend Hawthorne, is in stupid Art far gone;
Now when from real sculptors; works you stole,
That should fit snugly to his foggy soul,
'T is not unfair to think them and their labors
To Randolph Rogers and his work near neighbors.

The Nation's Capitol-extension is the one
For which those doors by Randolph Rogers have been done.
The Government is liberal; it has paid
Large sums for works of Art of such a grade,
That most of them worse could not well be made. (104)
Intrigue, or want of intrigue interpose
To let true merit show there what it knows.
ALLSTON, of all our painters the most thorough,
His way to this work could or would not burrow.
(But then the Boston millionaires contrive
A show of his works to keep him alive;
Two thousand dollars, ah! he gets by it,
Also from fear of fire a nervous fit)— (105)
But Billy Powells Congress circumvent
Obtain the work it for a native meant;
That they were not born here they can deny—
Suppose they do—that 's nothing but a lie!
I fear that Leutze's picture 's but addition, (106)
And with the rest comes into competition.
Leutze! 'gainst you I have some special rage
You may remember; also William Page.

'T is not presumptuous for me to declare,
That both should do your work with greater care.
Both of you able and both so reputed—
Tell me why by yourselves this is refuted!
Page I think always tries to do his best,
Though by some imps at times he seems possessed;
But rests there not on you a greater curse,
That brings your work from well to worse and worse,
Though singly almost, pictures fill your purse?
Somehow or other Art will bring a blight,
E'en change herself sometimes into a fright.
Young candidate for Art! would you still know
Why from this smoky town I do not go?
O'er all the Continent it is the same—
Art everywhere is blind and halt and lame,
And monster-humbugs gobble up the game.
What! go to England! yes, I see from here,
A sublunary Art-heaven there appear!
I see an insolent, proud commoner
To HAYDON play th' inhuman almoner;
See Haydon's spurting throat and spattered brain, (107)
Braggart civilization well sustain!
And TURNER fold his hands, die in despair,
Because they have the foul fool-critics there! (108)
If their Art-craving still proves insatiate,
See! Parliament, at an enormous rate,
Old Masters buys, and has the dirty fellows
Scrubbed, cleaned of all the skill that crudeness mellows;
For work like this men would on wheels be broken,
Had to mankind at large Art ever spoken.
Such mere brute-life is easily replaced,
But is the life from pictures thus erased?
Oh, Nineteenth Century! where 's more intense
Stupidity since time deigned to commence?
Such works of Art to all mankind belong—
Had books thus suffered, then we'd hear of wrong!

Ay, hear these very people howl at us,
And grow most impudently virtuous,
When Charleston harbor we would fill with stones— (109)
I wish it could be done with rebels' bones!

In the short history of our poor race,
Twice Art has had a dubious public place;
Then state-religion through Art's limits laid
The road to heaven for those they would degrade;
E'en then it never touched the great, live heart,
Of which the best of us must be a part
If we would live a life warm, active, bold,
Not in unsympathetic snow-drifts rolled.
Nay do not hope: it never will be better;
Bare backs and empty bellies still must fetter
The People's means; poor painters, sculptors live
On what the few rich whimsicals will give.
And here the worst of all this business lies:
Nowhere did education e'er comprise
A knowledge of the beauty bathing us—
Of Art that fain would be directing us—
Nowhere is it considered a disgrace,
Nothing to know of Art and Nature's face.
As Jefferson proved this when I began,
It shall be clinched now by a live statesman.
Of two great Presidents grandson and son,
'Mong statesmen left to us surpassed by none,
Of culture as we term it, ripe and rare,
CHARLES FRANCIS ADAMS, now in England, where (110)
Of these United States he has the care— —
He at Niagara pounced on the pictures
I made of it, and passed unasked his strictures;
Their color he was sure must be untrue,
Or if in Nature found, it would not do
To paint it so—I have forgotten why—
With few and flitting glances of his eye

His judgment 's final on my work at once,
He makes me as compared with him a dunce;
My young friend embryo-dauber, thus it stands:
I work all day with all my head, heart, hands—
For months, for years this water is my study;
Then Adams tells me that my mind is muddy—
Not in those words—for that he 's too polite,
He only says that I can not be right;
He gets his knowledge by God's bounteous grace,
While I with sweat and toil a phantom chase.
I question not his course as diplomat,
Or that, when Seward stirred him up somewhat,
He still most prudently John Bull should pat:
That Seward he should think too fiery—(ah!
Just what he said of our Niagara)
Nor do I doubt, when I take pains to see,
It is his business then to learn from me;
It is presumptuous unless he shows brains
That soak up knowledge without taking pains
To doubt results that I have not obtainèd,
Ere brain, eye, hand, heart long with care I trained.

That artist is of fool the synonym
Throughout society is not a whim.
The secretary of a petty company
Of fire-insurance, and my friend, coolly told me,
His work with hot brain-fever laid him low—
Then with his arm he made a flourish—so—
Mocking a dauber with his brush—" That 's play!
Could I like you be doing that all day!"
Poor fellow! then he'd get in no bad way!
Learned, illiterate, low, high, all are
In all affecting Art quite on a par.
See how they stare at me with blank surprise—
All, Byron-like, cry out why " we have eyes!"

Yes, and like him finely you use them too—
How the Medici Venus he can "do,"
With trim Canova cap the classic view! (111)
A dauber dare these sons of song sublime
Touch with his sneering and sarcastic rhyme?
Did they not tell me, my friends Bryant, Goddard, (112)
Whom with my lucubrations I had bothered,
One Michäel Angelo was but a jobber
In poetry—that that great sculptor-dauber
Wrote sonnets that were pretty good—that 's all—
Need I to th' inference attention call?

A part of my Niagara I read
To one who some time after to me said
That Byron's verses of St. Peter's pile (113)
Described Niagara in better style
Than aught he knew of: now they are to me,
With all their merit, phraseology,
Illogical applied to any thing—
Well, well, my lines may go for what they 'll bring.
I 'm glad that my conclusion 's near at hand—
If with my pen respect I can command,
I hope 't will prove my Art-work and the craft
Are not to be put 'mong the wholly daft.

Some of my friends think I keep back too much,
Ever of this world's cash my share to clutch.
It may be so; one knows not till one tries:
Since I would try all things, I advertise
To model and paint portraits, figures too;
Views of Niagara I'll furnish you,
And landscapes—all in any quantity—
You may yourself judge of their quality,
When told I paint and model as I write;
Take no advantage though of my bad plight,
Be liberal and be sure to pay *at sight.*

I wrote some things that I would like to sell
To a newspaper that will pay me well.
For this campaign—the Presidential—I would write,
In some way I would like for the great cause to fight;
My soul is in it, and I fairly burn
Copperheads, traitors on the spit to turn.
Still other ways and means I will devise:
I hereby for a Patron advertise;
No Littleworth, no Popkins need apply—
(Howe'er, of me perhaps such will be shy)—
But one whom money makes much more a man
Than honest poverty in this world can.
Through all the length and breadth of this great land,
Is there that man who 'll take me by the hand,
Who 'll say, keep at your work and I will see
That you have no small cash-perplexity—
Is there throughout civilization one?
Let him but speak—how soon will I say DONE.
Who wants Niagara—that splendid view,
With which this satire has so much to do,
Painted on canvas, six feet by fifteen,
Thus large to show the details we have seen;
The canvas is prepared and so am I,
With careful studies, now my brush to ply;
Who 'll give an order, pay half in advance—
Is there a moneyed man who 'll take this chance?
I must have two years time to paint it in,
Truth and completeness for the work to win.

Yes, I would linger in the Fine Arts' presence,
Their beautiful, their exquisite florescence.
More delicate, ethereal each day,
As if each moment it would flit away,
The common, beautiful, the olden, new,
Nature grows ever to my raptured view.

How pure and sharp are not those tints and lines;
But is there one that really defines
An end or a beginning or a place—
Impalpabilities each other chase!
I fear to touch with paint what seems a breath,
Looking as if a touch could cause its death,
And yet you feel that it but vails a force,
O'erwhelming in mysterious scope and source.
See from th' impalpable the palpable obtrude—
Look at that beauteous woman, God-made, nude—
Why to be looked at should she be afraid,
And why should you false modesty parade?
Her power as woman you may feel full well,
Her strange, dementating, enchanting spell,
Yet why not look at her e'en as a lover—
Of course then there is nothing here above her—
Not for earth's gold, its palaces, its lands,
Would you give one of those loved little hands!
And you are right—look at her! how she glows,
Each moment Nature novel charms bestows;
Flooded, not by the sun's sharp, linear light,
That seems for human flesh too strong, too bright,
But by that glorious glow around that orb,
When the clear sky can its great fire absorb;
This brilliant glow attempered by the blue,
Giving to human flesh its brightest hue—
Almost from angels tribute to demand,
Bathed in this glory, see the woman stand
On feet that are so wee, that are so weird,
Can they sustain the structure o'er them reared,
Whose swelling outline ceases not its scope
Till it clasps almost all earth's bliss and hope— —
Behold the greater beauty of the man—
It seems a shame to be but for a span;
How I have seen him leap and dive and swim,
Watched how the waves love-laved each supple limb;

What agile strength with highest beauty mated!
How thoughtlessly is woman overrated!
Poor Haydon says she 's handsomest, and then
His instinct gives us drawings but of men.
The curves that Ruskin calls the infinite,
(The finest line of beauty thus he hit)
Are well defined in man; in woman these
Approach the circular and—if you please—
Short-lived is woman's beauty if she give
What Nature must have that the race may live:
Though prodigal, destructive, Nature still
Her best work well to keep exerts some skill.
Beauty bedecks the male of bird and beast,
While the poor female always gets the least.
How firmly rest man's feet upon the ground—
How lithesomely they leave it on the bound!
Ay, it is meet that Beauty mate with Power!
From youth, to past the middle age, each hour
To well-made men should be one of content:
The power to punish the impertinent—
To give all dirty dogs a stunning blow,
Can any one a greater pleasure know?
Nay, do not talk to me of leveling laws—
Give me the strength to level, or to pause
And pass contemptuously the currish cause— —

And now once more, young candidate for Art,
I 'll speak to you that not like me you 'll smart.
I want, deserve no sympathy, for I
Was warned when a mere child, Art not to try.
They could not tell me though what else to do—
A panacea I have found for you.
If hewing wood and drawing water be
Beneath your high and mighty destiny,
If fancy-work you'd do, then take to writing;
'T is easier far than painting, more inviting

In all respects for profit and for pleasure,
And men will get much nearer to your measure.
Do not write novels, poetry, no! no!
Into the large arena you must go,
The printing-press and liberty have made—
Help those who use the pickaxe and the spade—
Write, that hard work the herd not more degrade!
Newspapers wield great and increasing power;
Here you can find some work for every hour;
Newspapers *are* read: you will get your pay,
And you can live thus in a manly way.
Small business you 'll find here; the Potter-grubs,
The handsome, heavy-headed Halstead-scrubs,
May get the place you ought to have; but still
Somewhere of paying work you 'll find a rill,
This in the mean Fine Arts you never will.
Mean as they are, they will not be degraded,
To love photography they can not be persuaded;
But local editors of papers may
Use the best language for what they would say;
If you have force you may climb upward thence,
As editor-in-chief to show your sense;
There honor, comfortable cash and power
You may secure, nor need you once to cower—
'T will teach you too to write at any hour.
Soul-stirring it must be to know your words
Gladden and move men's hearts like songs of birds,
Awakening them with joy to their hard task;
To mold their views could nobler part you ask?
If you *then* feel, good poetry to scribble
Is part of your vocation, take a nibble!

But see the Future of the press unfold!
What great and glorious work we there behold!
How well hath not fair Freedom lately sped—
Our odious oligarchy 's almost dead!

Millions of white and of black slaves are bounding
At once to freedom—the world's freedom rounding!
How ignorant, illiterate these are—
Would for their tyrants else 'gainst us they war?
E'en in the fields for freedom long since won,
How much, how much remains yet to be done!
Hunger and cold all men must keenly feel,
Relief from these is to all else the keel;
How radical the changes to be made,
Ere cold and hunger shall no man degrade.
Still we may doubt, with all drag-chains removed,
If mankind's folly be not ever proved;
No intellect seems and no training sure,
Inherent meanness of the race to cure.
Knowledge, religion, laws, all they 've invented,
Show them, how often! but the more demented.
The pound of brain above the average—
Lusus naturæ—gives the privilege
To be sometimes herein above the rest—
Non compos when it thinks it does its best;
The god-like sells his sense, his life, his soul,
To get where slavery willed a Polk should roll;
Though he flays with sarcasm puny Polk,
He'll pass, to reach Polk's place, beneath the yoke,
Then die as he deserves, his masters' joke.
Why will not men work for the work itself,
If they can live, why seek for office, pelf?
What is so valuable that men can give
Or God e'en, that man's manhood should outlive?
Is precious *life* not worthless if obtained
By means whose nature his pure nature stained?
See! Doctor SAMUEL JOHNSON, High Church Tory,
Whose name is blazoned with exceeding glory,
Whose trained mind reached that regal, rigid rule,
That must of tyranny be but the tool;

A famous moralist who never knew
Common politeness that was due to you.
DEAN SWIFT, who was a god compared with him—
Swift's great brain only water made to swim—
To spatter his last hours with lying spume,
This burly moral Johnson can presume.
He prick poor Swift for what was not a fault—
He dare that wreck—dare any one assault!
Of life itself, of friends, of money, fame,
He had enough ere death's slow summons came;
Now see him die! could we like him be blind,
And spare this low disgrace to poor mankind!
He shows when seventy and five years old
The worth of all the stuff he wrote and told;
Though sane as ever, how completely cracked:
Here *is* a show, a driveler! mangled, hacked, (114)
Hacked by himself to live, the fool must die,
While his mean soul gives to his creed the lie.

If great men are so wrong and are so weak,
When, where, for better things shall we then seek?
Or does the common herd in common sense,
Seem for less mind to find a recompense?
No matter: now occasion is at hand,
To try the People in supreme command,
And they have done well so far; therefore friend,
Drop palette, brushes, here a hand now lend—
To make and keep men's freedom pure and stable,
This cause needs all, all who are willing, able.
How many are there now this cause to flout—
Come! come! be at them! put them to the rout!
The President freed slaves by proclamation,
And that must be sustained by this great Nation.
Of the Supreme Court there need be no fear,
For if the People speak that court must hear.

Let all then go to work; now is the time;
To be indifferent to this cause is crime.
  In such a crisis where are Fine Arts, ah!
Seem they not then a great and wild *faux-pas?*
Till all get leisure, industry, desire,
To see the beauteous, exquisite attire,
The world we live in wears—until the soul
Can do without bread, shelter, clothing, coal,
Till then the Fine Arts are from life apart;
E'en if you 're rich, they may still crush your heart!
A universal language you would call
That which is understood by none at all?
To feel that no one wants what you can make,
May sometimes e'en the stoutest spirit shake;
At times her influence so soothing, tender,
Nature refuses utterly to render.
Niagara I love, yet all its power
Could not illume for me the horrid hour.

  Reader—to-night I would fain reach the close;
The hour has passed long since when the cock crows;
Dead silence is at rest, the wagons rattle,
And I suppose the pretty babies prattle,
Or cry—and soon we'll hear the cry of battle—
May victory to our bright banner come,
In *some* way may all traitors soon succumb.

  A few words more: by some I have been told
I swear too much in rhyming: do not scold;
Considering my subject well I think,
At this, if 't is a failing, you may wink.
Fuseli truly said it brought relief
If we are suffering from some sorts of grief.
Believe not though that I have carking care,
And hug the notion I have much to bear;

And do not so eggregiously mistake,
That ever aught but work keeps me awake.
I know not how these lines will be received;
If they 're not read I may not be much grieved.
I did my best; I spared no work, no time,
To say just what I meant in simple rhyme.
Ah! tell you what of all my stuff I think—
Tell that I used indelible—h'm! ink—
Nay, of its merit here I shall not prate:
But my paint-sculpture work I meant to vindicate;
It is my right to claim my just position—
Of self-conceit that is no exhibition—
You tell me all men talk so! do they, ah!
Yes—hear them, hear them at Niagara—
There on the same spot where we stood so long,
Sounding of self the laudatory gong!
"Nobody looking at this place would think
That *I* built all those houses!"—drink, drink, drink!
Drink self-conceit forever! can you fill?
Man! man! vain animal! you never will!
Three whitewashed shanties set up one by one,
Were the great work this man swelled up upon,
Where great Niagara is on the run.
  More ragged e'en than little Littleworth,
One of the sorriest sights I've seen on earth,
Though quite a young man, came and gave a view
Of all his toes and human nature too.
He brought some drawings of the Falls to sell:
I said, how you drew these I can not tell—
Then he poured out a torrent of conceit,
That Billem Sorry hardly could have beat;
"A gift of God!" he cried, "'t was with me born!"
I was astonished by this wight forlorn;
How voluble he was! glib! eloquent!
I thought his gaseous force would ne'er be spent;

He proved in using words there is a way
That sounds quite big and nothing has to say.
His drawings? well, nothing could be more queer,
Yet the brink's virile line did there appear;
(H'm! look for *that* in Church!) one was quite tragic—
A pig chased by a dog, as if by magic
Vanished behind a rock adown the cliff,
Showing his hinder parts, his tail, not stiff,
Not sticking up, but curling in that line,
Hogarth first showed us was so very fine,
That "line of beauty," best in well-tailed swine—
This fellow's genius though untaught had seized
These tail-twists just as if they were not greased,
This genius grasped these caudal convolutions,
E'en gave their complex, curious evolutions!
The foreground this: the distance showed the fall,
Which was like Church's, not a fall at all.

By nature great, ye NATURALS! ah could,
Could I speak of your merits as I would!
Great Billem Sorry, Church and our big Bones,
E. Barrett Browning, brother GRIFFIN JONES, (116)
The naturalest artist of the set—
One more whose name escapes me is well met,
Who modeled Washington and Liberty
Crowning and getting crowned, which you can see
Fenced in in Peter Cooper's Reading-room, New York; (117)
Why add more specimens? with these I close my work.
Immortals! of earth's one immortal race,
'Fore God and angels our great saving grace—
Imagine these, imagine all like them,
Together at Niagara—ahem!
When Art and Nature there their souls oppress,
Then may the waiting world look for a mess!
Now watch them! chattering, daubing, blind and deaf—
It seems miraculous—beyond belief!

But ha! whose antics! see them dance and grin!
Their laugh rings over the unceasing din—
Ha! mocking spray-sprites of Niagara,
We join your ha, ha, ha, ha, ha, ha, ha— —

NOTES

[1]The Cincinnati Pioneer Association was organized Nov. 23, 1856. Membership was open to the descendants of persons resident in the city before 1812, effectively excluding most German residents like the Frankensteins. Nicholas Longworth was one of the founders and served as president in 1858-59. In 1857 a monument honoring early settlers was proposed, and a location in Spring Grove Cemetery was donated for this purpose. Thomas Dow Jones submitted a design in October, 1863, but the monument was never erected. On April 7, 1860, William M. Corry delivered an address at the meeting of the Association. His speech is filled with grandiloquent praise of the pioneers, but there are no references to Jones and little or no resemblance to the speech imagined by Frankenstein.

[2]Thomas Dow Jones (Dec. 11, 1811-Feb. 27, 1881) was born in Oneida County, New York, but emigrated to Granville, Ohio, in 1837. After working as a stone mason and marble cutter in Cincinnati, he executed his first portrait bust in 1842; his subjects included Zachary Taylor, Lewis Cass, and other public figures. He was elected an associate of the National Academy in 1853. His Cincinnati studio was located at 47 East Fourth Street, just across the street from Frankenstein's. Jones was somewhat eccentric, experimented with perpetual motion devices, and occasionally wore a brigand hat and a Roman toga. He is best known for the Soldiers' Memorial in the Ohio Capitol, Columbus. In his old age he made a practice of standing beside this work and informing viewers that he had not been paid enough for it.

[3]William M. Corry (1811-80), a Cincinnati lawyer, was active in Democratic politics. During the Civil War the Cincinnati *Commercial* frequently attacked him as a Copperhead.

[4]Nicholas Longworth (Jan. 16, 1782-Feb. 10, 1863), founder of the Longworth fortune, an unpredictable Maecenas, and Frankenstein's *bête noire*, was born in Newark,

New Jersey. In 1803 he came to Cincinnati, where he read law. He accepted land in return for his legal services, and the rapid rise of real estate values soon made him wealthy. He assisted many Cincinnati artists, but his patronage did not include the Frankensteins.

[5]William A. Adams (July 3, 1797-Dec. 25, 1878), born in Boston, Massachusetts, was taken to Marietta, Ohio, by his parents in 1802. He read law in Zanesville and after 1840 practiced in Cincinnati. According to legend, he befriended Thomas Cole, then an itinerant painter, when the landlord of a Zanesville inn refused to accept a portrait of his wife in payment of a board bill. Adams was an amateur artist and also served as one of the supervisors of the construction of the Ohio State House in Columbus. The National Academy of Design is one of Frankenstein's primary targets.

[6]According to the Cincinnati *Commercial* for March 15, 1864, Griffin Taylor (1797-Dec. 22, 1866), a prominent Cincinnati merchant and banker, donated $200. to the Refugee Relief Commission of Ohio, a sum that Frankenstein apparently considered inadequate. Subsequent references in the poem indicate that he regarded Taylor as an enemy. A bust of Taylor by Thomas D. Jones (see Plate V) illustrates a compromise solution of the question whether public men should be represented by sculptors in togas or in contemporary dress.

[7]Lewis C. Hopkins (July 5, 1828- ?) was a merchant and real estate developer. He was an active supporter of the Sanitary Commission during the Civil War, and in January, 1864, paintings were sold at his store for the benefit of the Great Western Sanitary Fair (see n.98).

[8]R. C. Phillips (Jan. 13, 1834- ?), a surveyor, held several civic posts in Cincinnati. No reason for Frankenstein's animosity toward him is apparent except that he was assistant secretary of the Pioneer Association in 1863-64.

[9]A group of Cincinnati artists founded the Sketch Club in 1860. At each meeting the members would display illustrations of a literary work such as "The Deserted Village" or "Comus." In March, 1864, when Frankenstein completed his poem, the group held its monthly meeting at the studio of Thomas D. Jones.

[10]References in Part IV indicate that "Baby-booby" was a photographer. A purely conjectural identification would be Leon Van Loo, who was one of the most popular

Cincinnati photographers in 1864, also gave drawing and painting lessons, and was a member of the Sketch Club. His partner was William K. French.

[11]William H. Comstock was a wholesale merchant dealing in boots and shoes. Except for the incident described in this "dedication," no motive has been found for Frankenstein's animosity. In two letters to Lewis J. Cist of Cincinnati, written from Philadelphia Sept. 1, 1839, and Feb. 14, 1840 (Archives of American Art), Frankenstein sent his "compliments" to Comstock. Apparently this friendship, like most of his relationships, ended in bitterness.

[12]Thomas D. Jones spent part of January and February, 1861, in Springfield, Illinois, where he made a bust of Abraham Lincoln. He claimed (incorrectly) to be the only sculptor for whom Lincoln posed. In his *Memories of Lincoln*, not published until 1934, he recorded that Lincoln had asked Supreme Court Justice Noah B. Swayne, "Judge, what is that man's name in Ohio that makes mud heads?" The actor James E. Murdoch is also said to have told the story. Frankenstein's reference to it indicates that Lincoln's supposed remark was known in Cincinnati in 1863-64.

[13]The most succinct statement of Jefferson's utilitarian attitude toward the fine arts is his advice to two young friends planning to travel abroad: "Painting. Statuary. Too expensive for the state of wealth among us. It would be useless therefore, and preposterous, for us to make ourselves connoisseurs in those arts. They are worth seeing, but not studying." Quoted in Edward Dumbauld, *Thomas Jefferson, American Tourist* (Norman, Okla., 1946), p. 151.

[14]Frankenstein, of course, does not "faithfully report" Corry's oration, but puts his own sentiments into Corry's mouth. By not sustaining the Corry-persona, he weakens and confuses his satire. Apparently reporters skimmed this section of the poem after Frankenstein's death in New York City, because most of the obituaries stated that he had served in the Ohio Legislature, confusing him with Corry.

[15]Nicholas Longworth's mansion, Belmont, was built by Martin Baum in 1810. Longworth acquired it from the United States Bank in 1830. It is now the Taft Museum. Longworth engaged Robert S. Duncanson (see n.83) to paint a series of mural landscapes, and he also displayed numerous works by artist he had befriended.

[16]Thomas Buchanan Read (March 12, 1822-May 11, 1872) arrived in Cincinnati in 1837. He worked as a sign

painter and inscribed tombstones for Shobal Vail Clevenger (see n.27). After traveling throughout Ohio as an itinerant portrait painter, he established a studio in Cincinnati with the assistance of Nicholas Longworth. Although he lived in Philadelphia after 1846, he frequently visited Cincinnati, where his sister lived with her husband, Cyrus Garrett, a manufacturer of plows.

[17]Mrs. Browning's *Aurora Leigh*, first published in 1856, was widely admired in the United States. Perhaps Frankenstein disapproved of the mild feminism or of some of the incidental references to painting. A minor character, Vincent Carrington, an artist, is described as "bee-bonneted."

[18]Aaron H. Corwine (Aug. 31, 1802-July 4, 1830), born near Maysville, Kentucky, moved to Cincinnati in 1818. Dr. Daniel Drake and other Cincinnati citizens financed two years of study under Thomas Sully in Philadelphia. Best known for his portraits of Andrew Jackson and Lafayette, Corwine worked as a portrait painter in Cincinnati from 1820 to 1829.

[19]Possibly Louis M. Morgan (Nov. 21, 1814-1852), a portrait painter in Kentucky during the 1840s.

[20]James H. Beard (May 20, 1812-April 4, 1893) moved to Cincinnati from Painesville, Ohio, around 1835. Longworth considered him talented but indolent. He and his brother, William H. Beard, were successful portrait and genre painters, and all of his six children became artists. The most famous of them was Daniel Carter Beard, a founder of the Boy Scouts of America.

[21]In August of 1862, rumors spread through Ohio and Kentucky that General Kirby Smith planned to move on Cincinnati. General Lew Wallace was dispatched to the city, martial law was declared, and at least 60,000 citizen volunteers carrying a variety of weapons arrived. An army paymaster called them "the Squirrel Hunters," a term that has passed into Ohio legend. On September 12, the Confederate troops withdrew and the volunteers were dismissed. Both Beard and Read served as members of Wallace's staff. Read published an article, "The Siege of Cincinnati," in the *Atlantic Monthly*, February, 1863.

[22]Lilly Martin Spencer (Nov. 24, 1822-May 22, 1902), best known for her paintings of household scenes, children, and Shakesperean characters, was born in Exeter, England. Her father brought his family to Marietta, Ohio, in 1833. She was a protégée of Nicholas Longworth, who fi-

nanced her training in Cincinnati and offered to send her to Europe to study for seven years. She refused because he stipulated that she should copy the old masters and do no original painting while there. In 1847 she moved to New York City. Prints of her domestic genre paintings like "Shake Hands" (see Plate VI) were widely distributed by Goupil & Company.

[23]Alonzo Douglass (c.1815-1886), born in the District of Columbia, lived in Cincinnati and worked as a portrait painter for two brief periods, 1828-31 and 1842-46. Unable to support himself as an artist, he became a bank clerk in Kentucky.

[24]William Penn Brannan (March 22, 1825-Aug. 9, 1866) worked as a portrait painter in Louisville, Cincinnati, and other cities. He was also known as a poet and as a writer of humorous prose sketches. A collection of poems, *Vagaries of Van Dyke Browne*, contains a sonnet, "Jones' Bust of Lincoln," which would have been sufficient to arouse Frankenstein's resentment.

[25]William Henry Powell (Feb. 14, 1823-Oct. 6, 1879), born in New York City, was brought to Cincinnati as a small child. He studied under James H. Beard in 1836, and the next year Nicholas Longworth subsidized further training in the East. Powell is best known for "The Discovery of the Mississippi River by De Soto," which he painted for the Rotunda of the National Capitol. He also painted "The Battle of Lake Erie" for the Ohio Capitol Building. It was originally commissioned by the Ohio Legislature for a fee of $5,000. After completing the work in 1863, Powell requested $15,000 because of the unanticipated difficulty of the project; he eventually accepted $10,000. Frankenstein clearly suggests that the portrait of Corry was painted in return for his influencing the decision of the Legislature. Powell later created an enlarged replica of the painting for the U. S. Capitol (see Plate VII).

[26]Hiram Powers (July 29, 1805-June 27, 1873), the most famous and successful Cincinnati artist of Frankenstein's day, was born in Woodstock, Vermont, and came to Ohio in 1819. He worked in Watson's clock factory and later created animated wax figures and lurid spectacles with sound effects for the Western Museum (see n.88). In 1836 with financial assistance from Nicholas Longworth, he went to Washington, D. C., where he made portrait busts of President Jackson and other public men. The next year he sailed to Florence, where he passed the remainder of his life. He

corresponded regularly with his patron and named his son Longworth in his honor. "The Greek Slave" (see Plate VIII), which Powers completed in 1843, aroused considerable controversy over the question of nudity in art. Powers, whose talents were more mechanical than artistic, invented tools that polished marble so that it resembled flesh, resulting in what Frankenstein aptly calls "plastic portraiture." "The Greek Slave" was exhibited with great success in London in 1845 and in the United States two years later. Although Powers wrote that it was "not her person but her spirit that stands exposed," many Americans were shocked by the statue in spite of the coyly placed chain. In Cincinnati a private advance showing was held for a committee of clergymen, who concluded that the figure was "clothed in her own virtue" and approved it for public exhibition. An astute businessman, Powers later sold at least six replicas of the statue. The success of "The Greek Slave" and some of Powers' other statues such as "Eve Disconsolate" and "California" made the nude figure, if used for suitable narrative or allegorical effect, acceptable to the American public.

[27]Shobal Vail Clevenger (Oct. 22, 1812-Sept. 28, 1843), born near Middletown, Ohio, began working for a Cincinnati gravestone cutter in 1826. With no formal training, he determined to become a sculptor and produced excellent portrait busts of Henry Clay, Daniel Webster, and other public figures. In 1840 Longworth financed a trip to Europe for him and his family. He died of tuberculosis aboard ship while returning to the United States.

[28]John L. Whetstone (Aug. 30, 1821-May 1, 1902) was a portrait sculptor in Cincinnati, 1837-41. He abandoned art to become a mechanical engineer and a merchant. He was secretary and Godfrey Frankenstein was president of the short-lived Cincinnati Academy of Fine Arts, organized in 1838. The two men remained lifelong friends.

[29]William A. Adams (see n.5) was vice president of the Western Art Union (see n.35). Frankenstein's contention that he should not have displayed his paintings at the Art Union exhibition is based on the constitution of that organization, which stipulated a "Board of ten Directors, none of whom shall be professional Artists." Adams apparently argued that he was an amateur painter, not a professional, and therefore was elegible to exhibit. The 1850 report of the Board acknowledged that its activities had "been the subject of censorious animadversions during the past season," and Adams did not hold office again. Joseph Osgood Mussey

(1818-56) probably wrote the article in the *Gazette.* Frankenstein may have been nettled by the fact that Longworth purchased one of Adams' landscape paintings in 1849.

[30]Two copies of the poem (those in Illinois State Historical Library and Ohioana Library) contain the same marginal note beside this passage: Mrs. Wilson. The context suggests that she was the wife of a doctor, who perhaps was Frankenstein's landlord. She is probably the same Mrs. Wilson of Cincinnati who is described by Hannah Sawyer Lee in *Familiar Sketches of Sculpture and Sculptors* (Boston, 1854); this lady became enthusiastic about sculpture after visiting a studio, took up the art, and "worked with so much energy that sometimes she would faint away" (II, 217).

[31]William Karrman, a Cincinnati druggist, was one of the best known art collectors in the city. At the Great Western Sanitary Fair (see n.98), he exhibited a "collection of gems," water colors by European painters.

[32]Andrew Gano Burt (May 21, 1810-Jan. 28, 1875), a Cincinnati banker and art collector, suffered serious financial losses in 1861.

[33]Peyton Short Symmes (May 1, 1793-July 7, 1861) was not a professional artist but drew profiles and caricatures and also wrote prose and verse for Cincinnati periodicals. Dr. Lakey, who lent him some money, referred to him in his diary as "Peyton the Unready." In his autobiography, *Personal Memories* (Cincinnati, 1879), Edward D. Mansfield remarked on Symmes' fondness for puns and called him "the terror of the type-setters" because of his insistence on complete accuracy when any of his poems were published (p. 149).

[34]Samuel E. Foote (1787-1858) became wealthy as a merchant ship captain before he and his brother John P. Foote (1783-1865) settled in Cincinnati. There both men were involved in a variety of business enterprises and were active in the cultural life of the city. They persuaded their brother-in-law, Lyman Beecher, to move to Cincinnati to head Lane Seminary. Cubicles along the sidewalk in front of the Foote mansion at Third and Vine Streets were rented to artists, doctors, and lawyers (see Plate II). John and Godfrey Frankenstein shared a studio there in 1833. After Samuel Foote lost his fortune in the panic of 1837, ownership of the mansion passed to Griffin Taylor.

[35]Charles Stetson was president of the Western Art Union, which was modeled after the American Art Union in

New York City. This short-lived but influential attempt to popularize the work of American artists was first known as the Apollo Association when it was founded by an art dealer, James Herring, in 1838. Members paid $5.00 annual dues, which entitled them to a newsletter, an engraving, and a chance to win one of the works of art purchased with the income from dues. After James Gordon Bennett attacked the American Art Union as a lottery, a court decision forced it to disband in 1851, and its western counterpart followed suit. Before it was dissolved, the American Art Union had distributed over 2,000 original works of art and over 150,000 copies. Its brief but spectacular success probably encouraged many painters to turn from portrait painting to landscapes and anecdotal subjects. The Western Art Union rented rooms in a building at Fourth and Sycamore Streets in Cincinnati. In 1847 there were 724 subscribers; the following year, 1090; and in 1849, 1407. In 1850, when Hiram Powers' "Greek Slave" was announced as the major prize, the number of subscribers rose to 4724. Godfrey Frankenstein exhibited paintings in 1848, but no paintings by John are listed in the annual catalogues.

[36]General Prosper M. Wetmore (Feb. 14, 1798-March 6, 1876), a New York merchant and an amateur poet, was president of the American Art Union from 1847 until 1850, when he was succeeded by Abraham M. Cozzens (c.1810-Feb. 6, 1868). An officer in the state militia, Wetmore offended many artists by his arrogant manner.

[37]In 1838 an Academy of Fine Arts, one of several similar short-lived endeavors, was founded in Cincinnati with Godfrey Frankenstein as its first president. An exhibition at the Mechanics' Institute in 1839 was a financial failure.

[38]Frankenstein uses "Mrs. E" as a pseudonym for Sarah Worthington King Peter (May 10, 1800-Feb. 6, 1877), daughter of Ohio Governor Thomas Worthington. At the age of sixteen she married Edward King, son of Rufus King, U. S. Senator from Massachusetts. In 1831 they moved to Cincinnati, and Mrs. King made their mansion at Fourth and Vine Streets a gathering place for artists and writers. After her husband's death in 1836, she moved to Cambridge, Massachusetts. In 1843 she married the British Consul in Philadelphia, a Mr. Peter. After his death in 1853, she returned to Cincinnati. In 1854 she organized the Ladies' Gallery of Fine Arts and went to Europe to buy casts and copies of art works for the use of students. Much of the $9,000 raised for this project was supplied by Charles

McMicken, a Cincinnati merchant, who stipulated that the materials should revert to him if the Ladies' Gallery closed. They were later put in storage. He died in 1858, and in 1869 the trustees opened the McMicken School of Design in order to allow students to use the casts. In 1884 they were transferred to the University of Cincinnati and in 1887 to the Art Academy of the Cincinnati Museum. Strategic placement of fig leaves on nude statues was fairly common practice in the mid-19th century, but if an incident like the one described by Frankenstein ever occurred, it understandably passed unrecorded.

[39]James Fazzi is listed in the Cincinnati directory for 1856 as a maker of plaster statuary. In 1862 he occupied a studio in the same building as Thomas D. Jones.

[40]The Ohio Mechanics' Institute was incorporated in 1829. John P. Foote served as its president for nineteen years.

[41]Nicholas Longworth's father was a Loyalist whose property was confiscated during the Revolution. As a result Nicholas was apprenticed to a shoemaker in Newark, New Jersey. St. Crispin is the patron of shoemakers.

[42]Nicholas Longworth was singlehandedly responsible for the development of viniculture in Cincinnati. He experimented with native American grapes, the Catawba and Isabella varieties, and brought German specialists to Cincinnati to work in his vineyards. At the time of his death he was producing 150,000 bottles of wine a year. It was his custom to send complimentary cases of his product to public figures. Frankenstein may be referring to Longfellow, whose poem "Catawba Wine" (1854) was written in response to a gift of wine from Longworth.

[43]Dr. Charles Mackay (1814-89) visited Cincinnati in 1858 as the guest of the Burns Club. He wrote a series of letters about his American tour for the *London Illustrated News.* These letters when published by Harper in 1859 as *Life and Liberty in America* gave considerable offense to Southern slave-owners. Mackay praised Longworth at length for his "skill, enterprise, and public spirit" and for his "exertions in the cause of temperance and good wine." He called him "a man whom the Greeks would have apotheosized," quoted from the Longfellow poem, and praised Catawba wine. The last sentence of his discussion of Longworth illustrates the fulsome praise that irritated Frankenstein: "Nor is Hiram Powers the only artist whom the Western Bacchus has befriended, for Mr. Longworth uses his great

wealth to noble purposes, and never more willingly than in aiding the artist of genius up those few first steps of the ladder of fame which it is always difficult, and sometimes impossible to climb" (p. 139).

[44]George M. Dallas (July 10, 1792-Dec. 31, 1864) was American Minister to Great Britain, 1856-61. The incident to which Frankenstein refers was described by Longworth in a letter to Pliny Miles, a London botanist. He sent several cases of wine to Dallas, requesting that he turn them over to a wine merchant and keep a case for himself. Dallas regarded the request as an insult, refused to accept the shipment, and ordered it delivered to the American Consul, who "drank the wine without unpleasant feelings." Clara Longworth De Chambrun, *The Making of Nicholas Longworth* (New York, 1933), pp. 31-32.

[45]One of Longworth's eccentricities was his refusal to contribute to conventional charities and his liberality in assisting drunkards, prostitutes, and vagabonds, whom he called "the devil's poor." Every evening he held court in the basement of his home, where he received applicants for charity.

[46]Longworth died February 10, 1863, more than a year before Frankenstein published his poem.

[47]Frankenstein's bust of Supreme Court Justice John McLean (March 11, 1785-April 4, 1861), completed in 1857, is now in the Cincinnati Art Museum (see Plate IX).

[48]Norris R. Norton (1835-Dec. 18, 1870) served as a captain in Company K, 5th Ohio Cavalry, until the autumn of 1862, when wounded at Corinth, Mississippi. He is listed in the Cincinnati directory for 1863 as a journalist, and in 1864 he was a clerk employed by the Board of City Improvement.

[49]Charles Hammond (Sept. 19, 1779-April 3, 1840), lawyer and journalist, edited the Cincinnati *Gazette* from 1825 until his death. A conservative spokesman, he vigorously opposed the views and the actions of Andrew Jackson.

[50]Richard Smith (Jan. 30, 1823-April 22, 1898) moved to Cincinnati in 1841 and was for many years associated with the *Gazette.*

[51]Martin D. Potter(Nov. 19, 1819-April 4, 1866) was the publisher of the Cincinnati *Commercial*, the city's leading morning newspaper.

[52]Murat Halstead (Sept. 2, 1829-July 2, 1908) began as a reporter for the Cincinnati *Enquirer*, but was hired by

Potter to write for the *Commercial* in 1853. He was named editor-in-chief in 1859. A highly prolific journalist, he is said to have written a million words a year for forty years.

[53]Henry Reed (Nov. 25, 1809-Aug. 21, 1892) was on the staff of the *Enquirer* during the Civil War years. He lectured and wrote in favor of the toleration of slavery and of secession.

[54]James J. Faran (Dec. 29, 1808-Dec. 12, 1892) and Washington M'Lean (May 14, 1819-Dec. 8, 1890) were co-owners of the *Enquirer*, a Democratic newspaper often critical of the war effort and accused by many of Copperhead sympathies. Frankenstein undoubtedly is referring to a paragraph that appeared in the newspaper on April 26, 1862, dismissing the paintings on display in store windows "bearing the name of one or the other brothers Frankenstein" as "an advertising dodge" for Godfrey's panorama of Niagara. After ridiculing two of the pictures, the article praised several other Cincinnati artists, including Thomas D. Jones, "whose fame as a sculptor is known wherever art is appreciated." On March 8, 1863, an item in the *Enquirer* said of soldiers: "They will find their wives, perhaps, under the care of some charitable agent of an Aid Society who has found that there are more ways than one to administer consolation."

[55]Richard Crump (c.1805- ?), a portrait painter, worked in Kentucky around 1850, and Frankenstein may have known him at that time.

[56]John Locke (Feb. 19, 1792-July 10, 1865), a native of New Hampshire, founded a girls' school in Cincinnati in 1821, taught at the Ohio Mechanics' Institute, and was professor of chemistry and pharmacy at the Medical College of Ohio from 1835 to 1850. He also worked with David Dale Owen on some of his geological surveys. His praise of Godfrey Frankenstein was quoted in an advertisement for the Niagara panorama (Cincinnati *Gazette*, April 19, 1862).

[57]Robert Todd Lytle (May 19, 1804-Dec. 22, 1839) was a prominent Cincinnati citizen who served a term in Congress and was appointed Surveyor-General by President Jackson. The Lytle mansion, built in 1810 by his father, General William Lytle, was the first brick residence in Cincinnati. After completing his second term in 1837, Jackson was a guest there for two weeks before returning to Tennessee.

[58]William Haines Lytle (Nov. 2, 1826-Sept. 20, 1863) was wounded at Carnifex Ferry and again at Perrysville, where

he was taken prisoner. He was killed at Chickamauga, and an elaborate funeral was held in Cincinnati on October 22, 1863. An amateur poet, he was best known for "Antony and Cleopatra," a favorite declamation piece. Frankenstein obviously wrote some portions of this passage before Lytle's death.

[59]Northern admiration for General Thomas H. Jackson is one of many strange phenomena of the Civil War years. After his death on May 10, 1863, Cincinnati newspapers praised him highly. The *Enquirer* described him as "active, prudent and skillful" and praised his "military talent and intrepidity." The most famous instance of such glorification, of course, is Whittier's "Barbara Freitchie."

[60]Frankenstein is referring to the bitter gubernatorial campaign of 1863, in which John Brough defeated Clement L. Vallandigham, a Peace Democrat. Because of Vallandigham's anti-war speeches, General Burnside ordered his arrest on May 5, 1863. President Lincoln ordered that he be banished to the Confederacy, where he remained about three weeks. He conducted his campaign for the governorship from Windsor, Canada, and afterward returned to Ohio without interference. In the Presidential campaign of 1860, Vallandigham had vigorously supported Stephen A. Douglas.

[61]Friedrich Eckstein (c.1787-Feb. 10, 1852), "Father of Cincinnati Art," was born in Germany and came to Cincinnati in 1823. He founded a short-lived Academy of Fine Arts with John P. Foote as president of the board. He instructed and encouraged Hiram Powers.

[62]Alban Goldsmith (c.1788-1861) was born Alban G. Smith in Danville, Kentucky; his name was later changed to Goldsmith by an act of the New York Legislature. He studied surgery under Dr. Ephraim McDowell of Danville and in Paris. From 1833 to 1837 he taught surgery at the Medical College of Ohio, where Frankenstein is said to have studied anatomy. Deeply involved in controversies with Dr. Daniel Drake, head of the medical department of Cincinnati College, he left the city to lecture on surgery at the New York College of Physicians and Surgeons. He practiced genito-urinary surgery in New York until his death. Several medical reference books cite 1865 as the year of his death, but Frankenstein's lines indicate that 1861, as cited in Milton H. Thomas, *Columbia University Officers and Alumni 1754-1857* (New York, 1936) is correct.

[63]Johann Kaspar Spurzheim (Dec. 31, 1776-Nov. 10,

1832) popularized the pseudoscience of phrenology, originated by Dr. Franz Joseph Gall of Vienna. Phrenological societies were founded throughout the United States, and interest in the subject was widespread. Spurzheim died in Boston while on a lecture tour.

[64]Edward D. Mansfield (Aug. 17, 1801-Oct. 27, 1880), a journalist and civic leader, conducted a house-to-house canvass of the city to compile facts for *Cincinnati in 1826*. In the book he predicted that the Queen City would become a major metropolis. He emphasized the importance of the pork business, "perhaps not exceeded by that of any place in the world."

[65]Robert Fulton (Nov. 14, 1765-Feb. 24, 1815) painted portraits and miniatures; after 1793, when he turned to engineering, he painted only as a pastime. Samuel F. B. Morse (April 27, 1791-April 2, 1872) completed only one portrait after constructing his model telegraph in 1837. The remark about Morse not learning to paint is peculiar, because in 1811 he became a pupil of Washington Allston, the American painter Frankenstein admired most highly. Any artist who worked at Niagara Falls was Frankenstein's enemy, however, and Morse painted "Niagara Falls from Table Rock" in 1835. He may also have been influenced by the fact that in 1826 Morse was an organizer of the National Academy of Design, which he felt hampered American artists.

[66]Three artists named Darley (E. H., Felix O. C., and John C.), probably brothers, were exhibiting paintings in Philadelphia in the early 1840s while Frankenstein lived in that city. He undoubtedly refers here to Felix (June 23, 1822-March 27, 1888), who is best known for his illustrations of Cooper and Irving. Copies of his pictures were distributed to all members of the American Art Union. He was elected to the National Academy of Design in 1852.

[67]Erastus Dow Palmer (April 2, 1817-March 9, 1904), born in Pompey, New York, was best known for "The White Captive" (see Plate X), a nude statue completed in 1858. This work, for which his daughter modeled, achieved far greater warmth and lifelikeness than Powers' "Greek Slave," its obvious prototype. Largely self-taught, Palmer was the only important American sculptor of his generation not dominated by neo-classical influences. His group sculpture, "The Landing of the Pilgrims," designed for the U. S. Capitol in 1857, was rejected by Secretary of War John B. Floyd, who said that it portrayed an incident of only local interest.

[68]Charles Loring Elliott (Oct. 12, 1812-Aug. 25,

1868), born in Scipio, New York, after working as an itinerant painter for about ten years, lived in New York City, where he became a highly successful portrait painter. He was elected to the National Academy in 1846. Once a heavy drinker, he signed a temperance pledge, an action that Frankenstein apparently relates to his own reformation.

[69]The New York Sketch Club, founded in 1827, was inactive when Frankenstein wrote his poem; its last meeting was held in 1869. Most of the members also belonged to the National Academy of Design.

[70]Frankenstein's painting "Christ Mocked in the Praetorium" was highly praised. The Cincinnati *Gazette*, April 29, 1847, quoted a Philadelphia *Enquirer* article, calling it "a great picture, such as the old masters used to paint," and predicting that Frankenstein would "be enrolled among the genuine 'old masters' of our American school." The article closed with a notably inaccurate prophecy: "The West may well exult in the success of her favorite artist." Frankenstein also painted "Isaiah and the Infant Saviour." He remarks later in the poem that his "Christ pictures" brought many visitors to his studio but no purchasers.

[71]The half-line "And shut his dog out" appears in the First Book of *Aurora Leigh.*

[72]The three-story Studio Building at 43-55 West 10th Street, designed by Richard Morris Hunt, was built in the late 1850s. It contained galleries and numerous studios.

[73]William Hart (March 31, 1823-June 17, 1894), a landscape painter, born in Paisley, Scotland, and reared in Albany, New York, was elected a member of the National Academy in 1858.

[74]Emanuel Gottlieb Leutze (May 24, 1816-July 18, 1868), best known for "Washington Crossing the Delaware," was reared in Philadelphia, where Frankenstein may have known him briefly. He was a member of the National Academy and an occupant of the Studio Building.

[75]William Page (Jan. 23, 1811-Oct. 1, 1885), born in Albany, New York, one of the most popular painters of the day, was elected to the National Academy in 1837. When Frankenstein wrote, Page had recently returned from eleven years in Italy.

[76]Frederick Edwin Church (May 4, 1826-April 7, 1900), born in Hartford, Connecticut, was the only pupil ever accepted by Thomas Cole. Church exhibited with great success at the Art Union and was elected to the National

Academy in 1849. His best-known painting, "Niagara Falls" (see Plate XI), completed in 1857, attracted huge crowds when it was exhibited in New York, and John Ruskin praised it highly when it was shown in London the same year. Chromolithographs were widely distributed. The popularity of this painting of the Falls, which Frankenstein apparently regarded as the special province of his brother Godfrey and himself, aroused his scorn and inspired the prolonged and ineptly rapturous description of "the Lord's Niagara" that follows.

[77]On November 8, 1825, Samuel F. B. Morse presided at a meeting of young painters in rebellion against John Trumbull's imperious and high-handed direction of the Academy of Fine Arts. They formed the New York Drawing Association, which became the National Academy of Design, the most prestigious association of artists in America. By 1864 Frankenstein was probably justified in considering it conservative and monopolistic.

[78]General George B. McClellan held no command responsibility after November 7, 1862. By the time Frankenstein wrote his poem, he was associated with the Peace Democrats.

[79]George P. Shears was proprietor of the Clifton House at Niagara Falls. His son later moved to Cincinnati, where he operated the Grand Hotel and the Gibson House.

[80]Byron describes a waterfall in Canto Four of *Childe Harold's Pilgrimage*. The phrase "pitiless horror" occurs in Stanza LXIX.

[81]Judge Augustus Porter and his brother, General Peter B. Porter, were among the first settlers of Niagara Falls, then called Manchester. The family owned Goat Island from 1816 until 1885.

[82]George Loring Brown (Feb. 2, 1814-June 25, 1889), a native of Boston, lived abroad from 1840 to 1860. When Frankenstein wrote, his reputation as a landscape painter was at its height. According to Thomas W. Leavitt in "The Life, Work, and Significance of George Loring Brown" (Diss. Harvard 1957), pp. 110-111, Brown's painting of Niagara was completed in 1868; but in 1861 he visited the Falls to make studies for a winter moonlight view. Frankenstein must be referring to one or more of these preliminary studies.

[83]Robert S. Duncanson (c.1817-Dec. 21, 1872) began painting in Cincinnati in 1843. The Anti-Slavery League financed his study in Europe. His portrait of Nicholas Long-

worth (see Plate XII), also his benefactor, was painted in 1858. He exhibited a painting of Niagara Falls at the Great Western Sanitary Fair (see n.98).

[84]An unsigned article (written by Adam Badeau), "The Representative Art," in the June, 1860, issue of the *Atlantic Monthly* mentions Church and Turner in the same sentence but does not actually compare them. Frankenstein undoubtedly was annoyed by Badeau's central thesis—that music and drama were more representative of 19th century culture than painting and sculpture.

[85]The rather trivial incident that provoked this attack on the New York *Tribune* originated in the following note in the Cincinnati *Gazette* on September 10, 1860:

> The Marquis of Chandos has commissioned John and Godfrey Frankenstein to paint for him views of and at Niagara Falls. This is a high compliment to two of our Cincinnati artists, but we think it is deserved. The brothers Frankenstein have a great command of color, and a fullness of detail that mark them as conscientious, painstaking and accurate artists. John, especially, has not his superior among any modern artists whose works we have seen as a colorist. There is a wonderful brilliancy in his color. Godfrey has been long associated with Niagara. His "panorama" of the Falls was very successful as a work of art, and his views of Niagara have been much admired.

On September 22 the *Tribune* summarized this story and added that the Marquis of Chandos could not afford to commission paintings because the art treasures belonging to his father, the Duke of Buckingham, had recently been sold to pay his debts. There is no reason to suppose that this routine story was the work of the "art-editor" of the *Tribune*. In 1860 William H. Fry (1815-64), whose specialty was music, apparently was considered the art critic; but by 1863, when Frankenstein was writing, Clarence Cook (Sept. 8, 1828-June 2, 1900) had become notorious for his harsh, satirical criticism of painters. Frankenstein may have merged the controversy over Cook's criticism with his own earlier grievance.

[86]Frankenstein is referring to Greeley's former political alliance with Thurlow Weed and William H. Seward. They dominated New York State politics from 1838 to 1854.

[87]This attack on Poe is the most tantalizing and the most vicious section of the poem. Frankenstein lived in Philadelphia from 1839 to early 1844; Poe was also a resident

of the city during those years and wrote for a variety of periodicals. The most likely occasion for him to comment on Frankenstein's work would have been the annual shows sponsored by the Artists' Fund Society, where he exhibited one painting in 1841, six in 1842, and six in 1843. Except for two unfavorable notices in the Philadelphia *Public Ledger* (April 24, 28, 1842), Frankenstein was highly praised in Philadelphia newspapers and magazines. The *Saturday Courier*, which covered the exhibitions more fully than any other periodical, commenting on individual paintings in reviews extending through several issues, gave Frankenstein rather lavish notices. In 1841, when the severity of the *Courier* critic, under the pseudonym Claude, aroused public protest, Frankenstein was described as possessing "the true Promethean spark." Reviews in 1842 were favorable. The next year, however, the following comment on his "Portrait of a Lady and Child" appeared on April 22:

> There is great strength of character in the mother's face, but the child is very much distorted. Hogarth somewhere speaks of the line of beauty; it should be applied to children as well as to their parents. Mr. F. should remember that beauty in a work of art is, although not of the first, of some importance; he sacrifices too much to tone.

Neither the substance nor the style suggests Poe at his most casually journalistic. However, the review of the exhibition in the following issue of the *Courier* is followed by a "P," which Frankenstein may have thought designated Poe's authorship. Publication of Poe's "Gold Bug" in the *Courier* two months later may have persuaded Frankenstein that Poe was closely associated with the magazine and had attacked his painting. It is, of course, quite likely that Frankenstein blamed Poe for an unfavorable notice written by someone else, but the possibility remains that an unidentified Poe item awaits discovery in some Philadelphia publication. The violence of Frankenstein's denunciation of Poe may have been partially due to his close friendship with Willis Gaylord Clark (see Plate III), who had attacked Poe in the Philadelphia *Gazette & Commercial* (April 8, May 10, 1836). Clark's twin brother, Lewis G. Clark, editor of the *Knickerbocker Magazine*, was also unfriendly toward Poe, but their bitter feud did not fully ignite until after Poe moved to New York. At any rate, it seems probable that Frankenstein heard Poe discussed unfavorably among his circle of acquaintance in Philadelphia.

[88]Joseph Dorfeuille was curator of the Western

Museum, opened in 1820. To attract the Cincinnati public, he introduced wax figures, transparencies, and other devices. Hiram Powers and his brother were hired to repair figures that had been broken in transit and to create special effects. Frederick Franks, a Swedish artist, came to the city in 1825 and opened a museum over a drug store. A "Chamber of Horrors" attracted many patrons. At the suggestion of Mrs. Trollope, Dorfeuille met this competition with scenes from Dante's *Inferno*, a spectacle designated "The Infernal Regions." In 1835 Franks took over Dorfeuille's Western Museum, which he conducted until about 1860.

[89]Emerson depreciated somewhat the significance of art, considering it inferior to external reality, which in turn is inferior to unseen or spiritual reality. His reference to Newton occurs in his essay "Art": "I do not wonder that Newton, with an attention habitually engaged on the paths of planets and suns, should have wondered what the Earl of Pembroke found to admire in 'stone dolls.' "

[90]Frances Wright (Sept. 6, 1795-Dec. 13, 1852), born in Scotland, first came to the United States in 1818. The result of this trip was a book, *Views of Society and Manners in America.* In 1823 she accompanied or followed General Lafayette on his triumphal tour of America. Influenced by Robert Owen, she founded a community, Nashoba, in Tennessee. In July, 1828, after Nashoba failed, she delivered a series of lectures in the Hamilton County Courthouse, Cincinnati. In 1831 she married a French physician, Guillaume Sylvan Casimir Phiquepal D'Arusmont, whose adopted son was a brewer in Cincinnati. Although she traveled and lectured extensively on women's rights, abolition, and other reforms, Cincinnati remained her home until her death. No disclaimer such as Frankenstein mentions appears in *Views of Society* or in her published lectures.

[91]Nicholas Longworth.

[92]Richard L'Hommedieu (d. Jan., 1847) was publisher of the Cincinnati *Gazette.* "Exhibition pictures," as William Dunlap called them, many of them in the grandiose style of Benjamin West, were a major source of income for some painters. "The Court of Death," an immense allegorical "discourse on life and death" by Rembrandt Peale, was displayed throughout the United States for more than fifty years. In September, 1847, it was exhibited at Cincinnati College and later in the month at Melodeon Hall. The *Gazette* praised the painting almost every day and urged the public to attend. Frankenstein's memory apparently played

him false with respect to his conversation with L'Hommedieu, for the publisher was no longer living when the exhibition took place.

[93]Charles Soule (Sept. 2, 1809-March 30, 1869), born in Maine, was reared in Dayton, Ohio, and worked as a portrait painter in Cincinnati for several years. He was assisted by Longworth, who described him as "our best portrait painter" (Letter to Hiram Powers, Nov. 17, 1844. Cincinnati Historical Society).

[94]Photography was a flourishing business in Cincinnati. In 1856 the city directory listed eleven "Daguerrean Artists" and in 1864 thirty "Photograph Galleries." After an enlargement process was perfected, life-size portrait photographs with coloring supplied by a painter became highly popular. In a letter dated February 25, 1855 (Cincinnati Historical Society), the artist William Miller (c.1835-April 27, 1907) wrote to Isaac Strohm that he was working on "mezzographs" and that they would "revolutionize portraiture." The following passage from the same letter indicates Frankenstein's attitude:

> John Frankenstein dropped in to-day to see them, and appeared considerably exercised by what we showed him. He is puzzled to know what its effect will be on Art, but is inclined to think it will be highly detrimental. He has, however, always been "down" on Daguereotypes, so that his judgment is not impartial. He has frequently of late remonstrated with me about degrading my skill and attainments by coloring these pictures, and I have taken a somewhat malicious pleasure in decrying all portraiture as a mere mechanical performance and that this only reduces it to its proper level.

A column of "Art Gossip" in *Crayon* magazine (May, 1860, p. 141) praised Frankenstein as the only portrait painter in Cincinnati "who has never been guilty of painting photographs." Frankenstein may have been referring to the photographer Leon Van Loo as "Baby-booby" (see n.10).

[95]A notice in the Cincinnati *Gazette* (March 14, 1864) invited subscribers to John Frankenstein's painting of Niagara to meet at the Burnet House on the following day. On March 28 a similar notice appeared announcing a meeting of subscribers that evening.

[96]Frankenstein's studio was located at 14 East 4th Street. The identity of his landlord is uncertain.

[97]This confusing passage appears to refer to two legal

actions, which have not been identified; neither is listed in the daily court calendars published in Cincinnati newspapers. Both John and Godfrey Frankenstein painted portraits of various members of the Piatt family. A John H. Piatt was an attorney in Cincinnati in 1861, but his name does not appear in the city directory thereafter.

[98]After the success of a fair held in Chicago to raise money for the Sanitary Commission, Mrs. Elizabeth S. Mendenhall wrote to the Cincinnati *Times*, suggesting that Cincinnati could surpass Chicago's efforts. General Rosecrans accepted the presidency of the Great Western Sanitary Fair, which opened at Mozart Hall on December 22, 1863. When it closed on April 21 of the following year, its total receipts were $234,500. On exhibition were such "curiosities and relics" as the telescope used by Commodore Perry at the Battle of Lake Erie, the rope used by Colonel John Morgan to scale the wall of the penitentiary building in Columbus, and a beech chip bearing tomahawk marks made by Daniel Boone. The art gallery occupied three rooms next to this display. No paintings by John Frankenstein were exhibited. In fact, the success of this enterprise, his own exclusion from it, and the interlocking nature of the cultural establishment in Cincinnati may have motivated him to write his poem. Most of the local targets of his satire were involved in the Fair. He attacks all members of the Art Hall Committee: William Karrman, Thomas D. Jones, William P. Brannan, James C. Beard, and William A. Adams. Members of the Sketch Club displayed a series of paintings on the theme of war. Norris R. Norton contributed a poem, "The Foes of the Union." L. C. Hopkins, a member of the Executive Committee, displayed two statues by Randolph Rogers and a preliminary version of "Westward the Course of Empire Takes Its Way" by Leutze.

[99]At the Great Western Sanitary Fair, Thomas Buchanan Read (see n.16) displayed a three-quarter length painting of his friend, the actor James E. Murdoch. No portrait of Murdoch by Frankenstein has been located. A few months after Frankenstein wrote, on October 31, 1864, Read composed the only work for which posterity remembers him, the poem "Sheridan's Ride"; and Murdoch recited it that evening at Pike's Opera House, Cincinnati. George P. A. Healy (July 15, 1813-June 24, 1894), born in Boston, was one of the most successful American portrait painters of the 19th century. He exhibited at the Fair a three-quarter length picture of Longfellow painted in 1862. Frankenstein

is ridiculing the fact that Longfellow appears somewhat overdressed, wearing an overcoat and holding his hat in one hand and a cane in the other. Willis G. Clark arranged for Frankenstein to paint Longfellow's portrait in Philadelphia early in 1839. The painting has not been located. On April 21, 1839, Longfellow in a letter to Clark called Frankenstein "a fine fellow and a genius" Andrew Hilen ed. *The Letters of Henry Wadsworth Longfellow* (Cambridge, 1966), II, 140. Longfellow apparently suffered the same difficulties as some of Frankenstein's other sitters; after several months he wrote to Clark asking what had become of his portrait.

100Thomas J. Gallagher (d.March 11, 1876) was a lawyer and Democratic politician in Cincinnati.

101In Chapter XIV of *The Marble Faun* (1860), just before Kenyon, a sculptor from New England, shows Miriam his statue of Cleopatra, she expresses a hope that it is not a nude figure: "Every young sculptor seems to think that he must give the world some specimen of indecorous womanhood, and call it Eve, Venus, a Nymph or any name that may apologize for a lack of decent clothing. I am weary, even more than I am ashamed, of seeing such things. Now-a-days people are as good as born in their clothes, and there is practically not a nude human being in existence." She also says that "except for portrait-busts, sculpture has no longer a right to claim any place among living arts." Frankenstein probably also resented Hawthorne's remarks about artists' jealousy of each other and his statement that the truly creative work in sculpture was done by artisans hired by the master.

102"The White Captive" (see Plate X), a nude statue completed by Erastus Dow Palmer in 1858, was the subject of considerable controversy.

103In his Preface to *The Marble Faun*, Hawthorne wrote that he had attributed to Kenyon a bust of Milton, a statue of a pearl-diver by Paul Akers, and a statue of Cleopatra by William W. Story. In a brief reference to Randolph Rogers (July 6, 1825-Jan. 15, 1892), he said that he would also have appropriated his bronze doors "representing the history of Columbus in a series of admirable bas-reliefs, but was deterred by an unwillingness to meddle with public property." Rogers, who lived in Rome after 1855, completed the doors for the Capitol in 1858; they were cast at the Royal Bavarian Foundry in Munich. Frankenstein may have been angered by the fact that Rogers visited Cincinnati in December, 1862, was entertained by local citizens, and was commissioned to create a memorial monument, "The Soldier of the Line."

[104]Decoration of the extensions of the U. S. Capitol was first authorized in 1850; the selection of artists and subjects and, of course, the expenditure of public funds resulted in numerous controversies. After 1853 the work was under the supervision of the Secretary of War. Congressional authorizations usually specified that native American artists should be employed, but this stipulation was often disregarded. Much of the work was done by Constantino Brumidi of Italy (see n.117); others involved were Francis Vincenti of Italy, Charles Baudin and Horace Vernet of France, Albert Bierstadt and Emanuel Leutze of Dusseldorf, and Henry Domchowski, a Polish sculptor, who changed his name to H. D. Saunders.

[105]Washington Allston (Nov. 5, 1779-July 9, 1843) worked for more than twenty-five years on a huge painting, "Belshazzar's Feast." A group of wealthy Bostonians subscribed $10,000 to purchase the picture in advance and relieve him of financial worries. Instead, however, his obligation preyed on his mind; he continually altered and reworked the painting and worried about its being destroyed by fire. After his death it was found to be unfinished. Friends attempted to obtain Allston a commission for a painting in the Capitol, but he preferred Scriptural subjects. He considered for a time a painting of the landing of the Pilgrims.

[106]Emanuel Leutze painted "Westward the Course of Empire Takes Its Way" for the west staircase of the Capitol extension.

[107]Benjamin Robert Haydon (Jan. 25, 1786-June 22, 1846) is remembered today, if at all, for his friendship with Wordsworth, Scott, Keats, and other writers rather than for his massive historical and religious paintings executed in the "grand style." His most famous painting, "Christ's Entry into Jerusalem," was on display at the American Gallery of Painting in Philadelphia while Frankenstein lived in that city. Despondent and deeply in debt, Haydon committed suicide in his studio. He had been assisted financially by Lord Egremont and other patrons, but the "inhuman almoner" is probably Sir Robert Peel, who began befriending Haydon after his third imprisonment for debt in 1830. Haydon and his friends often complained of Sir Robert's parsimony.

[108]J. M. W. Turner (April 23, 1775-Dec. 19, 1851) was not fully appreciated during his lifetime, but his situation

was not as desperate as Frankenstein implies. His paintings made him moderately wealthy, and throughout the 1840s John Ruskin praised him extravagantly and vigorously defended his work.

[109]In late 1861 and early 1862, some Northern leaders were optimistic about the possibility of a "stone fleet," ships weighted with stones and sunk in Southern harbors. Twenty-five whaling ships were sunk in the principal channels of Charleston harbor, but they proved ineffective.

[110]Charles Francis Adams (Aug. 18, 1807-Nov. 21, 1886) was U. S. Minister to Great Britain during the Civil War years. Godfrey once painted his portrait, but there is no record of the encounter described here.

[111]*Childe Harold's Pilgrimage,* Canto Four, XLIX-LV.

[112]More than any other writer of his time, William Cullen Bryant was actively interested in the fine arts. He was a member of the New York Sketch Club, served as president of the American Art Union from 1844 to 1846, and was a close friend of Thomas Cole, Asher B. Durand, and other painters. Goddard cannot be identified precisely, but he apparently was a New York City professional man or merchant who occasionally visited Bryant in his office at the *Evening Post.* (William Cullen Bryant, II, Letter, Jan. 17, 1971.)

[113]*Childe Harold's Pilgrimage*, Canto Four, CLIII-CLX.

[114]"And Swift expires a Driv'ler and a Show." Samuel Johnson, "The Vanity of Human Wishes."

[115]The painter Henry Fuseli (Feb. 7, 1741-April 16, 1825) was notorious for his colorful profanity.

[116]Griffin Jones is not listed in any biographical dictionaries of artists, but he is referred to as an unskillful painter in a letter from William Miller to Isaac Strohm, February 25, 1855 (Cincinnati Historical Society).

[117]The Cooper Union Reading Room was opened November 2, 1859. No work of art like the one Frankenstein describes is mentioned in the early records of that institution; it may have belonged to an exhibition in the adjoining art gallery. Inexplicably, Frankenstein's description suggests "The Apotheosis of George Washington," a huge fresco in the dome of the U. S. Capitol begun in 1863 by Constantino Brumidi (July 26, 1805-Feb. 19, 1880) and completed in

1866. The Goddess of Liberty is on Washington's right and a figure representing Victory is on his left; he is surrounded by thirteen maidens, representing the original colonies. Perhaps a preliminary sketch of this work was displayed at Cooper Union.

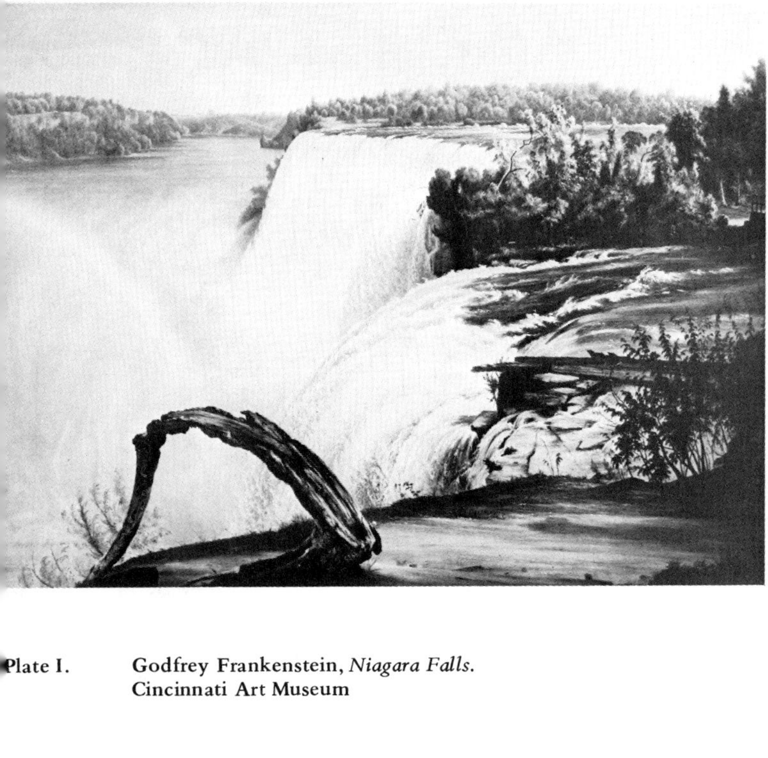

Plate I. Godfrey Frankenstein, *Niagara Falls.* Cincinnati Art Museum

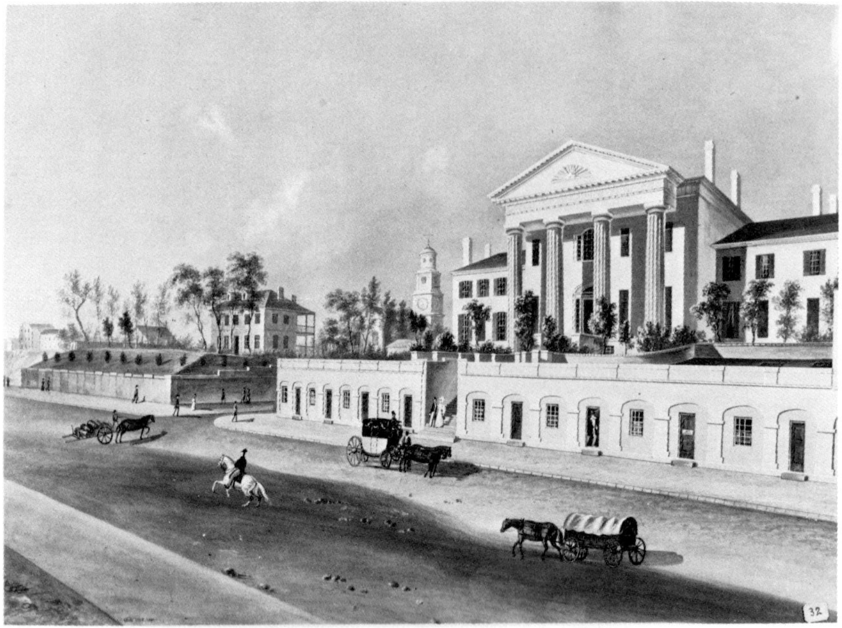

Plate II. John Caspar Wild, *Foote's Row*.
Cincinnati Historical Society

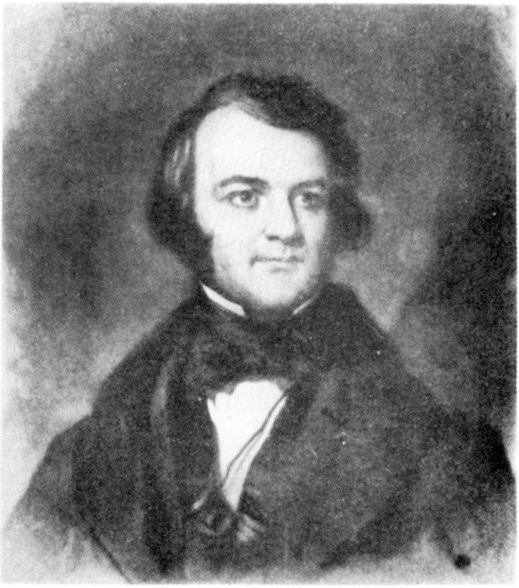

Plate III. John Frankenstein, *Willis Gaylord Clark.*
The Casket, Jan., 1840.
Reproduced from *The Letters of Willis Gaylord Clark*, ed. Leslie W. Dunlap. New York Public Library, 1940.

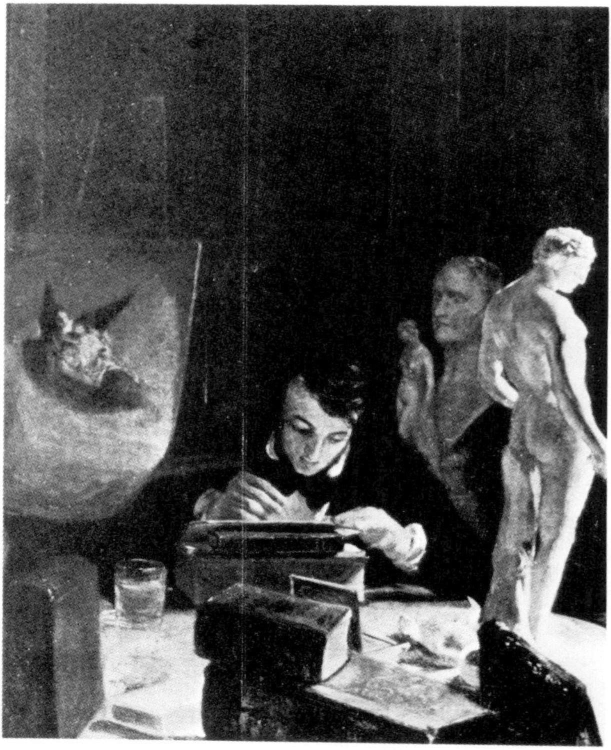

Plate IV. John Frankenstein, *The Artist in His Studio.* Victor D. Spark

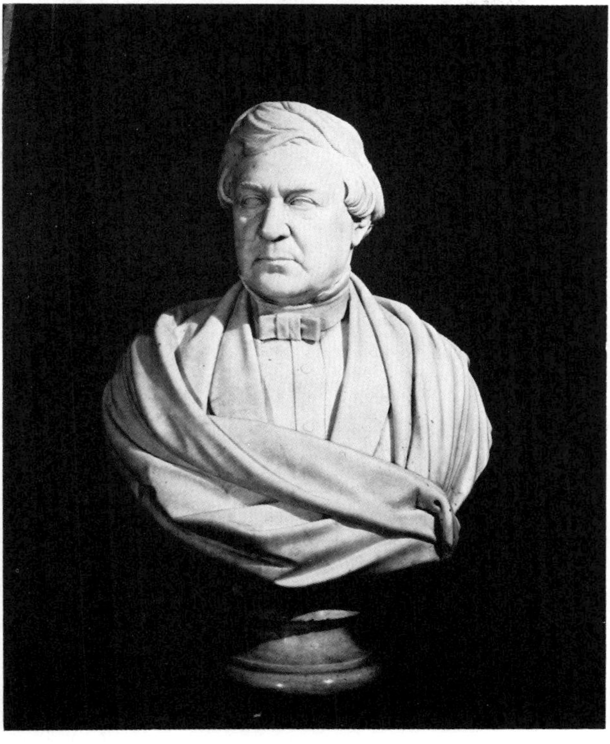

Plate V. Thomas D. Jones, *Griffin Taylor.*
Cincinnati Art Museum

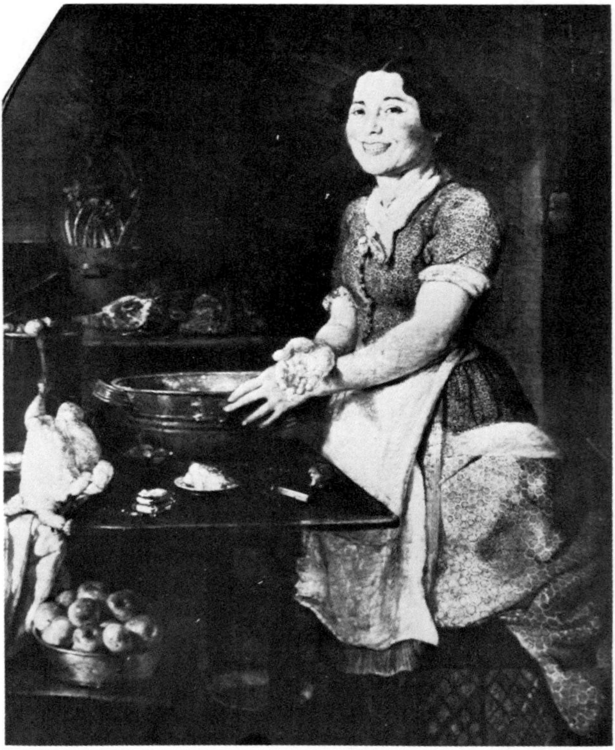

Plate VI. Lilly Martin Spencer, *Shake Hands.*
Ohio Historical Society Library

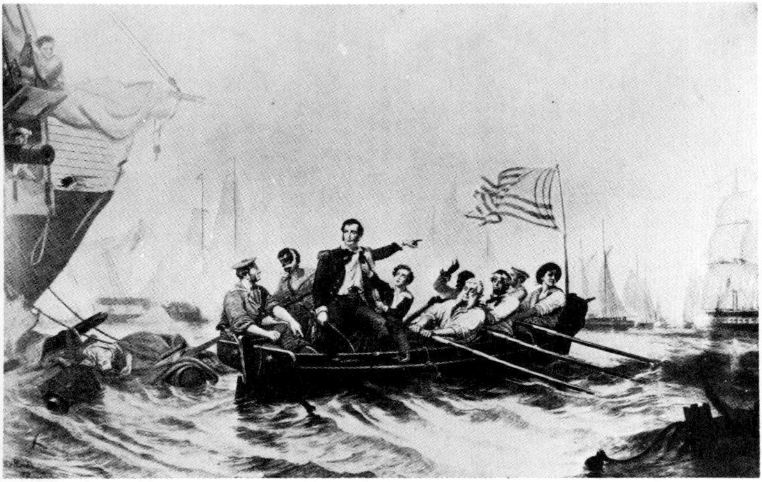

Plate VII. William Henry Powell, *The Battle of Lake Erie.*
U. S. Senate

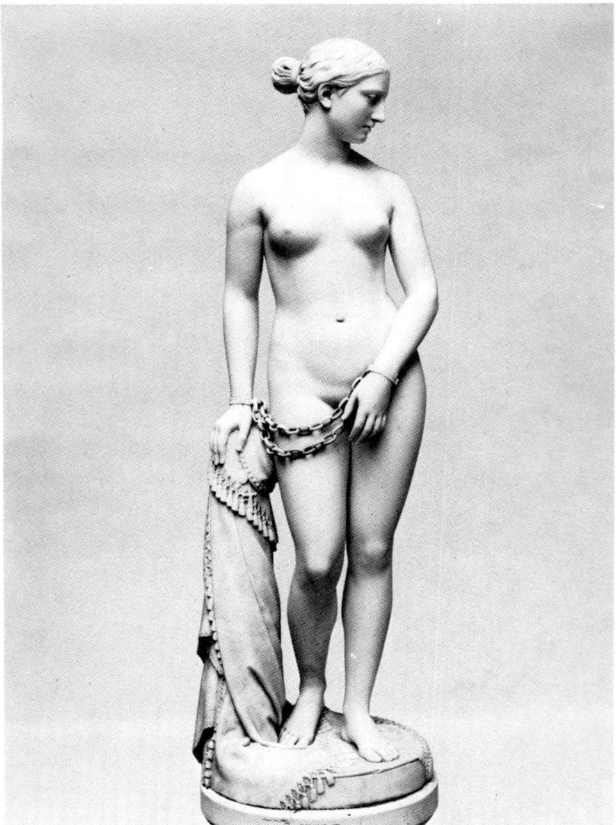

Plate VIII. Hiram Powers, *The Greek Slave.* Corcoran Gallery of Art.

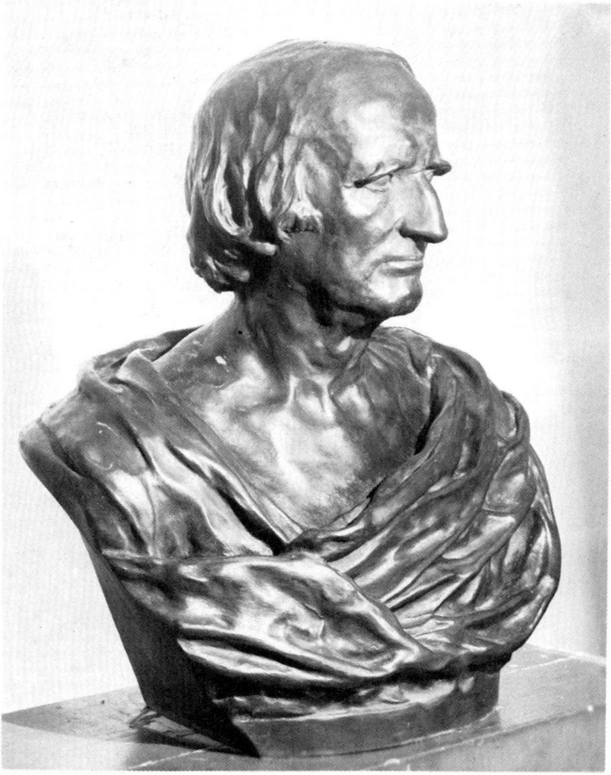

Plate IX. John Frankenstein, *Judge John McLean.* Cincinnati Art Museum

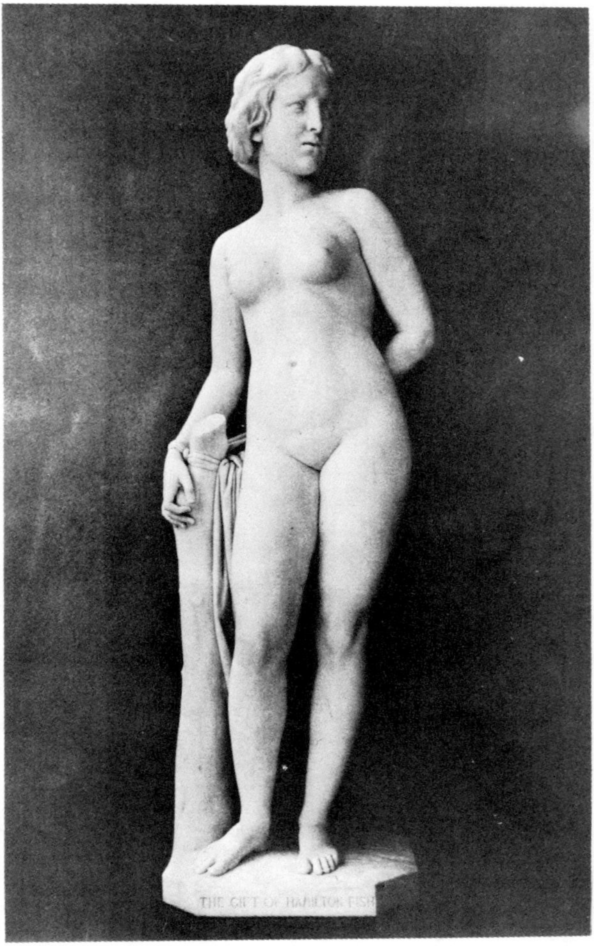

Plate X. Erastus Dow Palmer, *The White Captive.* Metropolitan Museum of Art, Gift of Hamilton Fish, 1894

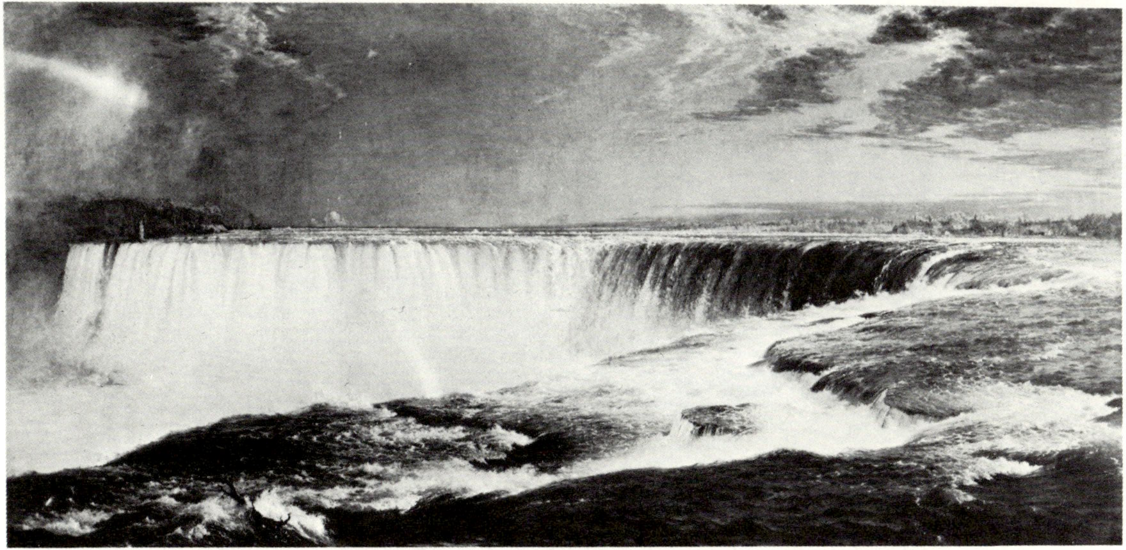

Plate XI. Frederick Edwin Church, *Niagara Falls.*
Corcoran Gallery of Art

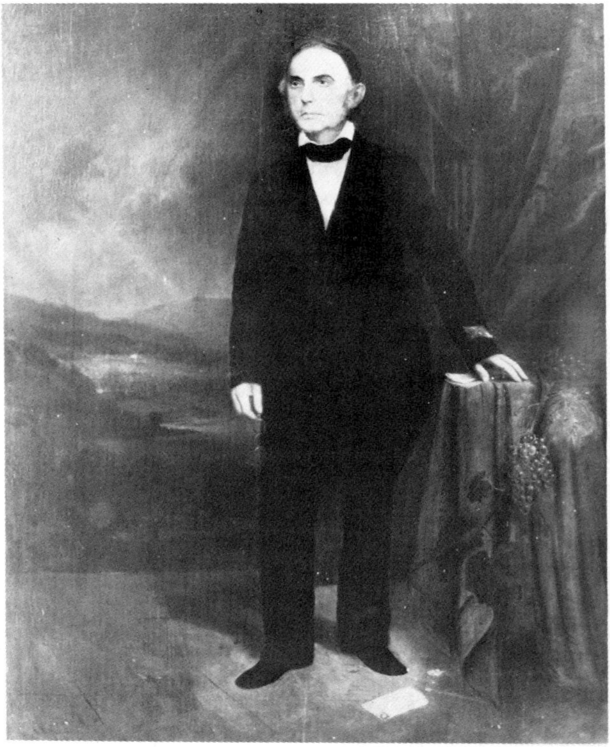

Plate XII. Robert S. Duncanson, *Nicholas Longworth.* Cincinnati Art Museum